Art & Otherness

Crisis in Cultural Identity

Thomas McEvilley

DOCUMENTEXT
McPHERSON & COMPANY

Published by McPherson & Company, Publishers, Post Office Box 1126, Kingston, New York 12401. Designed by Bruce R. McPherson. Typeset in Bembo by Delmas Typesetting, Inc. Manufactured in the United States of America. First Paperback Edition.
3 5 7 9 10 8 6 4 2

Library of Congress Cataloging-in-Publication Data

McEvilley, Thomas, 1939–
    Art & otherness : crisis in cultural identity / Thomas McEvilley.
       p.   cm.
    Includes index.
    ISBN 0-929701-21-6
    ISBN 0-929701-48-8
    1. Aesthetics, Modern—20th century.   I. Title.   II. Art and
otherness.
    III. Title: Cultural identity.
    BH39.M4344   1992
    701'.1—dc20   92-7120

Grateful acknowledgment is made to the publishers of earlier versions of essays comprising this book:
    "Introduction" in *Contemporanea*, 1990.
    "Revaluing the Value Judgment" (as "Critical Reflections"), "Doctor, Lawyer, Indian Chief," "The Common Air," "A Time to Change," "One Culture of Many Cultures" (as "Enormous Changes at the Last Minute"), and "The Global Issue," in issues of *Artforum* magazine.
    "ART/artifact: What Makes Something Art?," in *ART/artifact*, The Center for African Art, New York, 1988.
    "The Selfhood of the Other," in *Africa Explores*, The Center for African Art, New York, 1991.
    "Exhibitions, Real and Imaginary," in *L'Exposition Imaginaire*, SDU, Leiden, 1989.
    "Opening the Trap" in *Les Magiciens de la terre*, Centre national d'Art et de Culture, Paris, 1989.
    "The Romance: A Paradox" in *die Gleichzeitigkeit des Anderen*, Kunstmuseum, Bern, 1987.

The paper used in this publication meets the minimum requirements of American National Standard for Information Sciences—Permanence of Paper for Printed Library Materials.

CONTENTS

Art & Otherness

Introduction

In the first century AD, Strabo recorded [7.3.12] a
Scythian initiation rite in which youths would
dance in forest clearings clothed in wolf skins. After
bonding in this new identity they would regard non-
initiates as wolves' prey. It was an effective prepara-
tion for power struggles and war, as members of the
clan or tribal cult universalized their claim on power
by identifying with forces of nature. In the Modernist era, with its claims of universal standards of quality, the elite community of taste might have seemed
just such a group; certain artworks, especially those
of the abstract sublime, were its cultic emblems, like
wolf skins. The group for whom the work was made
was bonded around its secret meanings; and other
groups—*profani,* non-initiates, interlopers—were
rendered its social, economic, and cultural prey.
While seeming to emphasize universality or sameness, art in the West became a force for divisiveness
and exclusion.

With the gradual demise of Modernism during the
last three decades, however, there are signs that the
art world's cultic ambience is diminishing—or at the
very least that its membership base has broadened

dramatically. In the '50s and early '60s (the final heyday of Modernism) the range of art that could enter into art history was limited to, basically, abstract paintings out of Paris or New York by white male artists. In the '60s, first Pop art, then Minimal, Conceptual, and performance art loosened up the situation somewhat; by the '70s, the era that would be called pluralism, it was possible to make art in a variety of styles, and, even more epochally, women began entering the canon for the first time. As post-Modernism increasingly eroded the boundaries, the pluralism of the '70s expanded into the regionalism of the '80s: now it became possible to enter art history not only through a variety of styles but also from various places. One could be an artist in Texas or Australia and participate in the discourse that would become art history—but it still helped if one were a white male Westerner applying for cult membership; despite all claims of expansiveness, '80s regionalism did not include Kinshasa or Bombay.

These exclusions end in the globalism of the '90s, which is based on the recognition that art history as hitherto promulgated no longer coincides with the world we live in. To correct the fit, a fundamental shift in Western modes of cognition seems to be called for. During the Modernist period, Western anthropologists, despite admirable attempts at objectivity, tended to represent the rest of the world through Western conventions, as if the latter were normative, natural, or given. Western culture, taking its paradigm from its sciences, was to be the universal Self: non-Western culture was to be entirely Other. The idea of taking an anthropological approach to one's own culture—treating one's own culture as an Other—would have seemed subversive. Now, however, it is perceived that "otherness" is not a term associated with any particular ethnicity, but a universal: every group is "other" to every other group. The white male is as other to, say, the black female, as vice versa. Today, many Western anthropologists have come to see their goal as to shed light on their own culture as much as on others, light that must come, at least in part, from outside. To this end, they recognize the need to listen to voices previously excluded from the colloquy of the text or subordinated within it. The point of this exercise is the relativization of any one culture, the perception that it is not an absolute but just one approach among many to the shared human project of civilization.

Post-Modern critical modes of anthropology are paralleled by emerging critical tendencies in the art world. It now can be recognized that Modernist internationalism was a somewhat deceptive designation for Western claims of universal hegemony. In hopes of entering the international art discourse, a non-white or non-Western artist was to repress his or her inherited identity and assume a supposedly universal one; but that "universal" identity was just the emblem of another tribal cult that temporarily had the upper hand. Thus, Modernist internationalism was a form of imperial assertion by which non-Western cultures would assimilate to Western mores. But as Modernism fetishized sameness, post-Modernism fetishizes difference. A more genuinely global array of voices and visions comprises its project of cultural balancing. While it affirms cultural differences as too real to be ignored, this process also relativizes them, denying that any of them amounts to an absolute or universal, or can ever again pretend to such a transcendent status. As with dialogical anthropology, this project requires art to question and critique the very culture that produces it, rather than covering up that culture's weaknesses with a veneer of pleasing esthetic forms. Modernist art, by presenting beautiful objects lacking in apparent content, implied that the society producing such objects was also beautiful and also lacked hidden agendas or "contents." But if, after all, the social situation producing such art was not really so pretty, then the art must bear a lie within—as Blake said the rose has a worm in it. Criticism, once enchanted by the beauty of the rose, must now also attend to the worm.

At moments of intense social ferment, art can serve to retard, disguise, or misrepresent a society's potential for change. Today, against all odds, art is performing the opposite role. Tracking the future, it senses avenues along which a new self may emerge into the light of a redefined history. Shedding the wolf skin, it offers itself as a delicate, even tremulous ambassador to the world at large. It is still an intuitive antenna; but rather than intuiting other worlds and future transcendence into them, it senses the future face of *this* world and of an altered humanity to occupy it.

Many persons committed to the hegemonic claims characteristic of Modernism seem to feel threatened by globalization. In their eyes the deconstruction of Modernism in the '80s seemed nihilistic and profligate; post-Modernism's ridicule of the cult of originality, its aggressive mixing of high and low, its elevation of women and Third World artists to positions of prominence, its tendency to replace pure form with iconography, its rejection of traditional artisanal skills—these are among the frightening hints of the future they flee from. Above all, they are afraid that geo-cultural chaos will result if judgments of quality are seen as relative. The feeling seems to be like that of Plato, who, as a member of the aristocratic ruling class, felt that the original state of a thing is its primal perfection, and therefore that any change is degeneration. In this view, individuals' freedom of expression, as opposed to inherited types of communal expression, can only be disruptive, breaking up the totality of received wisdom. The forces of censorship today are similarly ill-disposed toward change. They want the visual realm to serve Western hegemony; they want art to make private emblems for a cult that does not vary. They want their wolf skin back.

But all judgments, in fact, are relative (to claim otherwise is to claim divine revelation), and a relative judgment is not necessarily unreal: it is limited only in applicability. As the conditions that produce them change, so judgments of quality change. Today, ideas of quality have been emerging which go beyond formal or esthetic matters to involve cognitive, social, and geographic ones: intelligence, wit, complexity, subtlety, surprise, honesty, critical incorporation of the contrary, sensed awareness of a particular location's resonances, the nesting of localities within localities to join one place to the rest of the world, just to mention a few.

Today's art can no longer be a holding action for the past. The current mandate is more in keeping with Jean-Francois Lyotard's remark that "art is a perpetual crisis."* As a map that shows us where we have been, and as a record that shows us who we were, surely art speaks about the past. But currently it has more to do with intuiting the future, squinting into its darkness for a glimpse of its unknown face. As cultural forces drift into new conformations that will not yet hold still long enough to be inspected, the artist proposes a sign system for the future that is necessarily dark, oracular, and ambiguous. His or her works are like banners set in a dim light in a dark field stretching to the horizon; their images, troubling or hopeful, beckon as they toss in fitful breezes of unknown origin.

The essays gathered in this book deal with these themes and more. In a sense, they are a record of the debate on multiculturalism and how it developed. They have a great deal to do with art exhibitions, which are the actual battleground where changes in art theory are currently being worked out. The dispute over the Museum of Modern Art's *"Primi-*

*Interview, "Handwriting on the Wall," *Contemporanea* 20, Sept. 1990, pp. 77–81.

tivism" show in 1984 was effectively the beginning of the discourse on multiculturalism in the realm of the fine arts. Five years later, *Les magiciens de la terre*, at the Centre Pompidou in Paris, was the first great counter-proposition. Some of my contributions to the debate are presented here, slightly edited for the continuity of argument, and with a few new notes added. "Doctor, Lawyer, Indian Chief" attacked the *"Primitivism"* show, and has been republished in several languages. "Opening the Trap" is adapted from the keynote statement for the *Magiciens* catalogue. "The Global Issue," presented here as an appendix, contrasts these two exhibitions and their journalistic receptions. Some consequences of the end of Modernism are discussed in "Revaluing the Value Judgment," "One Culture of Many Cultures" and "A Time to Choose." "The Common Air: Contemporary Art in India," excerpted here from a more detailed *Artforum* essay, investigates the complicated diffusion and reception situation existing between the West and the contemporary culture of India. The appendix "ART/artifact: What Makes Something Art?" originated as part of an exhibition colloquium at the Center for African Art, New York, which explored the ramifications of the *"Primitivism"*/*Magiciens* dichotomy. "The Selfhood of the Other" appeared first as a catalogue essay for an exhibition of contemporary art from Africa, also at the Center for African Art. "The Romance: A Paradox" was written first for a catalogue of the 1987 exhibition, *The Simultaneity of the Other*, at the Kunstmuseum in Bern, Switzerland.

Revaluing the Value Judgment

The mainstream tradition in Western philosophy—what Richard Rorty has called the Plato-to-Kant axis—has argued for universal and unchanging criteria of quality that are supposedly valid for all times and places. There are differences in expression—Plato spoke about objective universals and Kant about subjective universals—but it is a shared idea that correct judgments are based on a correct perception of universals, and incorrect ones on a misperception of them. Absolute values, in this view, are inborn in all humans identically in all times and places, in what Plato called the Eye of the Soul, and what Kant called the Faculty of Judgment, or Taste. Some people can apprehend these inborn ideas clearly, and some, because of a variety of obscuring factors, cannot.

This belief implicitly underlay the most influential Modernist art criticism from Roger Fry to Clement Greenberg, critics who felt, and were able to convince others, that they had an especially clear ability to perceive these universals. Though Fry is dead and

Greenberg retired, the attraction of the universals is still formidable. Even if they don't articulate it, the most outspoken proponents of the priority of quality over all other issues in art today still assume this theoretical foundation, which is particularly associated with neo-conservatism and the opponents of so-called political correctness.

Even the partisans of universals should have to respond to issues of reasoning and evidence, and there is nothing that could be called evidence suggesting that quality is objective and universal, rather than subjective and relative. There is, however, abundant evidence on the other side of the question. First, there is the historical evidence: the simple fact that taste changes over time. Countless examples could be invoked to illustrate this; we're all familiar with them. Artists seen as great by their own generation may seem mediocre to a later one, and vice versa. The very notions of what makes a work good have been observed to change from age to age.

If quality is to be regarded as an unchanging universal even though the idea of quality frequently changes from one age to another, then one or the other age, or both, must simply be wrong. In fact, since no past age has had quite the idea of quality that prevails today, it would follow either that we are wrong in our judgments or that all past ages were wrong in theirs. Faced with this dilemma, and unable to take the former alternative seriously, classical Modernists tacitly affirmed the latter, however preposterous it might seem. Indeed, it was supported by the classical Modernist belief in progress, a belief involving the idea that all past ages were essentially striving to become what we now are. Yet it is hard really to imagine what it would mean to say that the peoples of the past were somehow "wrong" when they lived their lives upon the earth as we are now living ours. If, on the other hand, we accept that quality is relative and shifts as time passes, then each age may be regarded as right in its time and in its way.

There is a second avenue of approach to the question, not through history but in terms of cultures that coexist in time. Here again one sees striking regional variations in the notion of quality. The idea of a "good" picture changes from Kinshasa to New York to Beijing to Alice Springs. The same alternatives that followed from reflections on historical change follow here: either some cultures are right and others wrong, or quality is not an unchanging universal but a subjective reality projected outward onto things.

The classic Modernist solution, which was characteristic of the colonialist era, was essentially to say that every culture but ours was wrong. Nowadays that opinion seems to reflect a chillingly, even tragically flawed self-absorption. To be objective rather than subjective, such a judgment would have to be made in some extra-cultural place with a clear view of every culture, including our own—a view unavailable from within any culture. Clearly, no such vantage point is available to human beings. The alternative, which has gained currency recently, is to say that the reality of quality changes from culture to culture, as it does from age to age, and that no culture's—or age's—idea of quality can claim a universal validity. Since no body of observable evidence has ever been adduced for the idea of universality, I see no escape from this conclusion except wishful thinking.

This idea, however, makes many people deeply unhappy. Some feel that it leads to a chaos in which subjectivity reigns to such an extent that discourse becomes impossible. Connoisseurship, and the cultural hierarchies that rest on it, are eliminated in turn. Finally, the fear goes, by giving up the idea that our own quality judgments are universal, we end by somehow betraying our own culture. I think these views are mistaken, and furthermore that they go against their own intentions by treating our culture as fixed and rigid, as if it were obsolete, before that moment in fact has come.

By recognizing the fluctuations in the idea of quality we are not abandoning the quality discourse, merely setting its limits. The situation that follows is not in fact chaotic, for the history of connoisseurship suggests that quality judgments do have a degree of stability within limited contexts of time and space. People in the same culture, with the same education and the same class background, living at the same time in history, may well have similar ideas of quality. This is no small fact. Actually, it saves the idea of quality, because it means that value judgments are still to be regarded as meaningful among the members of any of the conditioned groups from which a society is constituted. This opens the door far enough for the culture of connoisseurship to come in. That an informed viewer of, say, Modernist abstract paintings (or, for that matter, baseball cards) should have a better sense of what it is appropriate to call a "good" example of the genre than an uninformed viewer is not in question here; "good" in this context means simply what a consensus of informed viewers would agree on. And they *would* agree, loosely, which shows that something real is going on in the value judgment, though this reality seems not to be an objective perception of universals.

It seems clear that we take as objective measures of value what we have been conditioned to take that way. This is not so simple as it might sound, however, because there are a lot of conditioning factors involved. One of these is the cultural tradition in which one lives. In the Western tradition in general, for example, any art that rises from the Greco-Roman lineage (and, even more broadly, the Sumero-Egyptian) looks recognizable as art and thus will correspond to some degree to our tradition of connoisseurship. Alongside the conditioning influence of tradition are factors such as social class; region, too, has an impact, with inhabitants of certain regions of the United States, say, more likely to appreciate country-and-western music than inhabitants of others. This is not a matter of someone being right and someone else being wrong. It's a matter of the framework shifting around the act of judgment.

Gender, age, occupation, and physical and mental health also underlie and shape value judgments. Even within relatively small, highly defined groups, such as, say, the members of a particular college class, there will be differences based on individual neurotic formations—one person's desire to agree with his or her parents, another's desire to disagree with them, and so on. The conditioning situation does not mean that all members of one culture will agree, like identically programmed robots, but that the set of options available within a given culture, though complex, is still limited. It is also important to acknowledge that conditioning can be amended and expanded by people trying to educate themselves and to pursue their interests, and that a culture's set of mental options is always changing and always to some degree up for grabs.

At the same time, however, the forces that control the society around us, powerful conditioning agents in themselves, can be depended upon to use their position to advance their own program. Hence, value judgments are subject to the influence of forces like what Theodor Adorno called the Culture Industry, and what Louis Althusser called Ideological State Apparatuses. A society's prevailing value system is in part a concealed ideological tool. (The famous use of Abstract Expressionist painting as what Eva Cockcroft called a weapon of the Cold War is one conspicuous example.) All value judgments, being historically conditioned, are partly motivated ideologically and thus are susceptible to social change, but it is to the advantage of the controlling group to posit its own criteria as eternal and universal.

This does not mean that these criteria are invalid; the powers that be, to make their system as convincing as they can, are apt to make use of the most highly focused sensibilities in the service of bonding society around the structure they desire. And a value judgment, though not a universal, is still a very real expression of a culture's sensibility, an avenue to the appreciation of what might be called its personality or soul—understanding this to be a changing and contingent entity. The relativized position thus does not betray the integrity of a culture. It bears repeating, however, that the Platonic-Kantian tradition performs class service, and that its invocation usually signals a defense of power.

I am not advocating that we dispense with the value judgment—I am not sure how we could. But we could become more self-conscious in our exercise of it, and, ultimately, could learn to make new uses of it. First, we have to criticize our own tastes and to see that certain elements in them are local and temporary and have hidden motivations that are not necessarily honorable. Second, we should learn to relativize our own value judgments, to see them as arising from certain circumstances, and to see that other circumstances would give rise to different ones.

So what are value judgments *for?* Socially, they serve to define and bond groups—communities of taste—in ways that are often useful and always dangerous, because by bonding some people they exclude others. Because of this danger there is an urgency to the whole question; for when one community of taste attempts to enforce its idea of quality on another, an irrational and dangerous act is performed that can only arise from hidden, perhaps violent motives.

Aside from this function, judgments of quality seem to serve some of the legitimate needs of individual selfhood. The pleasure of exercising judgment is a pleasure of self-realization, self-recognition, and self-definition. One reflects oneself, and contemplates the reflection of oneself, by bouncing one's radar of appreciation off of this and that, rejecting this, rejoicing in that, putting certain things in a class with oneself, excluding others from it, and so on.

I think that this process could be converted into a social force with far greater usefulness if it were pushed further than we are accustomed to do. Usually, we experiment with our appreciation radar in childhood and early adulthood, then rigidify around the results. This is what we like, and who we are, forever. Behind this rigidification of taste is an assumption of universality not necessarily articulated. We feel that to change a preference we held in the past would be to admit that we had been wrong. But when the idea of universality is abandoned, this issue disappears. We realize that from the point of view we once held, such and such a judgment was valid, but from a different point of view which we now hold, another becomes valid. Yet we can understand both points of view at once, and therein lies the key.

Through a deliberate extension of this ability, the act of self-recognition can grow into an act of expanded self-creation. By learning to appreciate the value stance of groups other than the one we were born into, we in effect expand our selfhood. In this piecemeal way we can approach the project of becoming not universal in a metaphysical sense, but global in a more pragmatic sense—I mean the sense of incorporating, through deliberate effort, some feeling of what is meant when an Indian, or a Japanese, or a Senegalese, or an Australian says this or that is good.

To me it seems that this is the whole point of our present confrontation with the idea of the value judgment: that there are ways in which this human activity can be used far more sanely and helpfully than it has been used in the past, and that this moment is our great opportunity to articulate them and put them into practice.

Doctor, Lawyer, Indian Chief

"Primitivism" in Twentieth Century Art
at the Museum of Modern Art

Something clearly is afoot. Richard Oldenburg, director of the Museum of Modern Art, describes one of its publications and the exhibition it accompanies, both titled *"Primitivism" in Twentieth Century Art: Affinity of the Tribal and the Modern* [1984], as "among the most ambitious ever prepared by The Museum of Modern Art." "Over the years," he continues, "this Museum has produced several exhibitions and catalogues which have proved historically important and influential, changing the ways we view the works presented, answering some prior questions and posing new ones."[1] Indeed, this *is* an important event. It focuses on materials that bring with them the most deeply consequential issues of our time. And it illustrates, without consciously intending to, the parochial limitations of our world view and the almost autistic reflexivity of Western civilization's modes of relating to the culturally Other.

The exhibition, displaying one hundred fifty or so Modern artworks with more than two hundred tribal objects, is thrilling in a number of ways. It is a tour de force of connoisseurship. Some say it is the best primitive show they have seen, some the best Eskimo show, the best Zairean show, the best Gauguin show, even in a sense the best Picasso show. The brilliant installation makes the vast display seem almost intimate and cozy, like a series of early Modernist galleries: it feels curiously and deceptively unlike the blockbuster it is. Still, the museum's claim that the exhibition is "the first ever to juxtapose modern and tribal objects in the light of informed art history"[2] is strangely strident. Only the ambiguous word "informed" keeps it from being ahistorical. It is true that the original research associated with this exhibition has come up with enormous amounts of detailed information, yet since at least 1938, when Robert Goldwater published his seminal book *Primitivism in Modern Painting,* the interested public has been "informed" on the general ideas involved.[3] For a generation at least, many sophisticated collectors of Modern art have bought primitive works too, and have displayed them together. For five or so years after its opening in 1977, the Centre Pompidou in Paris exhibited, in the vicinity of its Modern collections, about a hundred tribal objects from the Musée de l'Homme. Though not actually intermingled with Modern works, these were intended to illustrate relationships with them. More recently, the exhibition of the Menil Collections in Paris' Grand Palais, in April, 1984, juxtaposed primitive and Modern works (a Max Ernst with an African piece, Cézanne with Cycladic, and so on). The premise of this show, then, is not new or startling in the least. That is why we must ask why MoMA gives us primitivism now—and with such intense promotion and such an overwhelming mass of information. For the answer, one must introduce the director of the exhibition and, incidentally, of the museum's Department of Painting and Sculpture, William Rubin.

One suspects that for Rubin the Museum of Modern Art has something of the appeal of church and country. It is a temple to be promoted and defended with passionate devotion—the temple of formalist Modernism. Rubin's great shows of Cézanne, in 1977, and Picasso, in 1980, were loving and brilliant paeans to a Modernism that was like a transcendent Platonic ideal, self-validating, and in turn validating and invalidating other things. But like a lover who becomes overbearing or possessive, Rubin's love has a darker side. Consider what he did to Giorgio de Chirico: a major retrospective of the artist's work in 1982 included virtually no works made after 1917—though the artist lived and worked for another half-century. Only through 1917, in his earliest years as an artist, did de Chirico practice what Rubin regards as worth looking at. This was a case of the curator's will absolutely overriding the will of the artist and the found nature of the oeuvre. A less obvious but similar exercise occurs in Rubin's massive book *Dada and Surrealist Art*[4]—a book not so much about Dada and Surrealism as against them. The Dadaists, of course, and following them the Surrealists, rejected any idea of objective esthetic value and of formally self-validating art. They understood themselves as parts of another tradition which emphasized content, intellect, and social criticism. Yet Rubin treats the Dada and Surrealist works primarily as esthetic objects and uses them to demonstrate the opposite of what their makers intended. While trying to make anti-art, he argues, they helplessly made art. Writing in 1968, at a time when the residual influence of the two movements was threatening formalist hegemony, Rubin attempted to demonstrate the universality of esthetic values by showing that you can't get away from them even if you try. Dada and Surrealism were, in effect, tamed.

By the late '70s, the dogma of universal esthetic feeling was again threatened. Under the influence of the Frankfurt thinkers and of post-Modern relativism, the absolutist view of formalist Modernism was losing ground. Whereas its esthetics had been seen as higher criteria by which other styles were to be judged, now, in quite respectable quarters, they began to appear as just another style. For a while, like Pre-Raphaelitism or the Ashcan School, they had served certain needs and exercised hegemony; those needs passing, their hegemony was passing also. But the collection of the Museum of Modern Art is predominantly based on the idea that formalist Modernism will never pass, will never lose its self-validating power. Not a relative, conditioned thing, subject to transient causes and effects, it is to be above the web of natural and cultural change; this is its supposed essence. After several years of sustained attack, such a credo needs a defender and a new defense. How brilliant to attempt to revalidate classical Modernist esthetics by stepping outside their usual realm of discourse and bringing to bear upon them a vast, foreign sector of the world. By demonstrating that the "innocent" creativity of primitives naturally expresses a Modernist esthetic feeling, one may seem to have demonstrated once again that Modernism itself is both innocent and universal.

"Primitivism" in Twentieth Century Art is accompanied by a two-volume, 700-page catalogue, edited by Rubin, containing more than a thousand illustrations and nineteen essays by fifteen eminent scholars.[5] It is here that the immense ideological web is woven. On the whole, Goldwater's book still reads better, but many of the essays here are beautiful scholarship, worked out in exquisite detail; Jack Flam's essay on the Fauves and Rubin's own hundred-page chapter on Picasso exemplify this strength. The investigation and reconstruction of events in the years from 1905 to 1908 recur in several of the essays: these years constitute a classic chronological problem for our culture, like the dating of the Linear B tablets. At the least, the catalogue refines and extends Goldwater's research (which clearly it is intended to supplant), while tilling the soil for a generation of doctoral theses on who saw what when. Its research has the value that all properly conducted scientific research has, and will be with us for a long time. In addition to this factual level, however, the catalogue has an ideological, value-saturated, and in-

terpretive aspect. The long introductory essay by
Rubin establishes a framework within which the
other texts are all seen, perhaps unfortunately. (Some
do take, at moments, an independent line.) Other
ideologically activated areas are Rubin's preface and
Kirk Varnedoe's preface and closing chapter, "Contemporary Explorations" (Varnedoe is listed as
"codirector" of the exhibition after "director" Rubin).

A quick way into the problems of the exhibition
is in fact through Varnedoe's "Contemporary Explorations" section. The question of what is really contemporary is the least of the possible points of con-
tention here, but the inclusion of great artists long
dead, like Robert Smithson and Eva Hesse, does suggest inadequate sensitivity to the fact that art-making
is going on right now. One cannot help noting that
none of the types of work that have emerged during
the last eight years or so is represented. Even the
marvelous pieces included from the '80s, such as
Richard Long's *River Avon Mud Circle,* are characteristic of late '60s and '70s work.

A more significant question is the unusual attention to women artists—Hesse, Jackie Winsor,
Michelle Stuart, and above all Nancy Graves.
Though welcome and justified, this focus accords
oddly with the very low proportion of women in the
show that preceded *"Primitivism"* at the new MoMA,
*An International Survey of Recent Painting and Sculp-
ture.* That show had a different curator, yet in general it seems that curators need a special reason to
include a lot of women in a show—here, perhaps the

association of women with primitivism, the unconscious, and the earth, a gender cliché which may
have seemed liberating ten years before but may
seem constricting ten years hence.

In the context of Modern art, "primitivism" is a
specific technical term: the word, placed in quotation
marks in the show's title, designates Modern work
that alludes to tribal objects or in some way incorporates or expresses their influence. "Primitivist," in
other words, describes some Modern artworks, not
primitive works themselves. "Primitive," in turn,
designates the actual tribal objects, and can also be
used to denote any work sharing the intentionality
proper to those objects, which is not that of art but
of shamanic vocation and its attendant psychology.
Some contemporary primitivist work may loosely
be called primitive;[6] yet the works selected by Varnedoe are conspicuously non-primitive primitivism.
The works of Smithson and Hesse, for example,
may involve allusion to primitive information, but
they express a consciousness highly attuned to each
move of Western civilization. Rubin and Varnedoe
make it clear that they are concerned not with the
primitive but with the primitivist—which is to say
they ask only half the question.

There are in fact contemporary artists whose intentionalities involve falling away from Western civilization and literally forgetting its values. These are
the more nearly primitive primitivists; they are edited out of the show and the book altogether. The
furthest the museum is willing to go is Joseph Beuys.
Varnedoe explicitly states a dread of the primitive,

referring darkly to a certain body of recent primitivist work as "sinister" and, noting that "the ideal
of regression closer to nature is dangerously loaded,"
that such works bring up "uncomfortable questions
about the ultimate content of all ideals that propose
escape from the Western tradition into a Primitive
state."[7] The primitive, in other words, is to be cen-
sored out for the sake of Western civilization. The
museum has evidently taken up a subject that it lacks
the stomach to present in its raw realness or its real
rawness. Where is the balance that would have been
achieved by some attention to work like Eric Orr's
quasi-shamanic objects involving human blood,
hair, bone, and tooth; or Michael Tracy's fetishes of
blood, hair, semen, and other taboo materials? The
same exorcising spirit dominates the schedule of live
performances associated with the exhibition: Mere-
dith Monk, Joan Jonas, and Steve Reich, for all their
excellences, have little to do with the primitivist and
less with the primitive. Where are the performances
of Hermann Nitsch, Paul McCarthy, Kim Jones, and
Gina Pane? Varnedoe's dread of the primitive, of the
dangerous beauty that attracted Matisse and Picasso
and that continues to attract some contemporary artists today, results in an attempt to exorcise them and
to deny the presence, or anyway the appropriateness,
of such feelings in Western humans.

Our closeness to the so-called contemporary work
renders the incompleteness of the selection obvious.
Is it possible that the classical Modern works were
chosen with a similarly sterilizing eye? Was primitive
primitivist work made in the first third of this cen-

tury, and might it have entered this exhibition if the Western dread of the primitive had not already excluded it from the art history books? Georges Bataille, who was on the scene when primitive styles were being incorporated into European art as Modern, described this trend already in 1928, as Rosalind Krauss points out in the catalogue's chapter on Giacometti. He saw the estheticizing of primitive religious objects as a way for "the civilized Westerner ... to maintain himself in a state of ignorance about the presence of violence within ancient religious practice."[8] Such a resistance, still dominant in this exhibition almost sixty years later, has led not only to a timid selection of contemporary works but to the exorcising of the primitive works themselves, which, isolated from one another in the vitrines and under the great lights, seem tame and harmless. The blood is wiped off them. The darkness of the unconscious has fled. Their power, which is threatening and untamed when it is present, is far away. This in turn affects the more radical Modern and contemporary works. If the primitive works are not seen in their full primitiveness, then any primitive feeling in Modernist allusions to them is also bleached out. The reason for this difficulty with the truly contemporary and the truly primitive is that this exhibition is not concerned with either: the show is about classical Modernism.

The fact that the primitive "looks like" the Modern is interpreted as validating the Modern by showing that its values are universal, while at the same time projecting it—and with it, MoMA—into the future as a permanent canon. A counterview is possible: that primitivism on the contrary invalidates Modernism by showing it to be derivative and subject to external causation. At one level this show undertakes precisely to co-opt that question by answering it before it has really been asked, and by burying it under a mass of information. The first task Rubin and his colleagues attempt, then, is a chronological one. They devote obsessive attention to the rhetorical question, Did primitive influence precede the birth of Modernism, or did it ingress afterward, as a confirmatory witness? It is hard to avoid the impression that this research was undertaken with the conclusion already in mind. The question is already begged in the title of the exhibition, which states not a hypothesis but a conclusion: *"Primitivism" in Twentieth Century Art: Affinity of the Tribal and the Modern.*

The central chronological argument, stated repeatedly in the book, is that, although the Trocadero Museum (later the Musée de l'Homme) opened in Paris in 1878, primitive influences did not appear in Parisian art until some time in the period 1905 to 1908. This thirty-year lag is held to show that the process of diffusion was not random or mechanical, but was based on a quasi-deliberate exercise of will or spirit on the part of early Modern artists—in Rubin's words, an "elective affinity."[9] It was not enough, in other words, for the primitive images to be available; the European receptacle had to be ready to receive them. As far as chronology goes, the argument is sound, but there is more involved than that.

What is in question is the idea of what constitutes readiness. Rubin suggests that the European artists were on the verge of producing forms similar to primitive ones on their own account—so positively ready to do so, in fact, that the influx of primitive objects was redundant. For obvious reasons, Rubin does not spell this claim out in so many words, yet he implies it repeatedly. For example, he writes that "the changes in modern art at issue were already under way when vanguard artists first became aware of tribal art."[10] The changes at issue were of course the appearances of primitive-like forms. The claim is strangely improbable. If one thinks of Greco-Roman art, Renaissance art, and European art throughout the 19th century, there is nowhere any indication that this tradition could spawn such forms; at least, it never came close in its thousands of years. A counter-model to Rubin's might see readiness as comprising no more than a weariness with Western canons of representation and esthetics, combined with the gradual advance, since the 18th century, of awareness of Oceanic and African culture. The phenomena of art nouveau (with its Egyptianizing tendencies) and *japonisme* filled the thirty-year gap and demonstrate the eagerness for non-Western input that was finally fulfilled with the primitive works. Readiness, in other words, may have been more passive than active.

Clearly, the organizers of this exhibition want to present Modernism not as an appropriative act but as a creative one. They reasonably fear that their powerful show may have demonstrated the op-

posite—which is why the viewer's responses are so
closely controlled, both by the book and, in the
show itself, by the wall plaques. The ultimate reason
behind the exhibition is to revalidate Modernist esthetic canons by suggesting that their freedom, inno-
cence, universality, and objective value are proven
by their "affinity" to the primitive. This theme has
become a standard in dealing with primitivism;
Goldwater also featured the term "affinities," rather
than a more neutral one like "similarities."

A wall plaque within the exhibition informs us
that there are three kinds of relations between Modern and primitive objects: first, "direct influence";
second, "coincidental resemblances"; third, "basic
shared characteristics." This last category, referred
to throughout the book as "affinities," is particularly
presumptuous. In general, proofs of affinity are
based on the argument that the kind of primitive
work that seems to be echoed in the Modern work
is not recorded to have been in Europe at the time.
Ernst's *Bird Head,* for example, bears a striking resemblance to a type of Tusyan mask from the upper
Volta. But the resemblance, writes Rubin, "striking
as it is, is fortuitous, and must therefore be accounted
a simple affinity. *Bird Head* was sculpted in 1934, and
no Tusyan masks appear to have arrived in Europe
(nor were any reproduced) prior to World War II."[11]
The fact that the resemblance is "fortuitous" would
seem to put it in the category of coincidental resemblances. It is not evidence but desire that puts it in
the "affinities" class, which is governed as a whole
by selection through similarly wishful thinking. In

fact, the Ernst piece cannot with certainty be excluded from the "direct influences" category, either. The argument that no Tusyan masks were seen in Europe in 1934 has serious weaknesses. First of all, it is an attempt to prove a negative; it is what is called, among logical fallacies, an *argumentum ex silentio,* or argument from silence.[12] All it establishes is that Rubin's researchers have not heard of any Tusyan masks in Europe at that time. The reverse argument, that the Ernst piece shows there were probably some around, is about as strong.

A similar argument attempts to establish affinity between Picasso and Kwakiutl craftspeople on the basis of a Kwakiutl split mask and the vertically divided face in *Girl Before a Mirror,* 1932. For, says Rubin, "Picasso could almost certainly never have seen a 'sliced' mask like the one we reproduce, but it nonetheless points up the affinity of his poetic thought to the mythic universals that the tribal objects illustrate."[13] The argument is weak on many grounds. First, Picasso had long been familiar with primitive art by 1932, and that general familiarity, more than any "universals," may account for his coming up with a primitive-like thing on his own. The same is true for Ernst and the *Bird Head.* Modern artists don't necessarily have to have seen an object exactly similar to one of their own for influence to exist. Anyway, the similarity between *Girl Before a Mirror* and the "sliced" Kwakiutl mask is not really that strong. The mask shows a half head; the girl has a whole head with a line down the middle and different colors on each side. Rubin attempts to correct this weakness in the argument by noting that "Northwest Coast and Eskimo masks often divide integrally frontal faces more conventionally into dark and light halves."[14] But most of the world's mythological iconographies have the image of the face with the dark and light halves. Picasso had surely encountered this common motif in a variety of forms—as the alchemical Androgyne, for example. There is, in other words, no particular reason to connect his *Girl Before a Mirror* with Kwakiutl masks, except for the sake of the exhibition.

In addition to Rubin's reliance on the notoriously weak argument from silence, his "affinities" approach breaches the Principle of Economy, on which all science is based: that explanatory principles are to be kept to the smallest possible number *(entia non multiplicanda sunt praeter necessitatem)*. The Principle of Economy does not of course mean keeping information to a minimum, but keeping to a minimum the number of interpretive ideas that one brings to bear on information. The point is that unnecessary principles will usually reflect the wishful thinking of the speaker and amount to deceptive persuasive mechanisms. In the present case, ideas like "elective affinity," "mythic universals," and "affinity of poetic thought" are all *entia praeter necessitatem*, unnecessary explanatory principles. They enter the discourse from the wishful thinking of the speaker. An account lacking the ghost in the machine would be preferred. The question of influence or affinity involves much broader questions, such as the nature of diffusion processes and the relationship of Modernist esthetics to the Greco-Roman and Renaissance tradition. In cultural history in general, diffusion processes are random and impersonal semiotic transactions. Images flow sideways, backwards, upside down. Cultural elements are appropriated from one context to another not only through spiritual affinities and creative selections, but through any kind of connection at all, no matter how left-handed or trivial.

The museum's decision to give us virtually no information about the tribal objects on display, to wrench them out of context, calling them to heel in the defense of formalist Modernism, reflects an exclusion of the anthropological point of view.[15] Unfortunately, art historians and anthropologists have not often worked well together; MoMA handles this problem by simply neglecting the anthropological side of things. No attempt is made to recover an emic, or inside, sense of what primitive esthetics really were or are. The problem of the difference between the emic viewpoint (that of the tribal participant) and the etic one (that of the outside observer) is never really faced by these art historians, engrossed as they seem to be in the exercise of their particular expertise, the tracing of stylistic relationships and chronologies. The anthropologist Marvin Harris explains the distinction:

Emic operations have as their hallmark the elevation of the native informant to the status of ultimate judge of the adequacy of the observer's descriptions and analyses. The test of the adequacy of emic analyses is their ability to generate statements the native accepts as real, meaningful, or appropriate. . . . Etic operations have as their hallmark the elevation of observers to the status of ultimate judges of the categories and concepts used in descriptions and analyses. The test of the adequacy of etic accounts is simply their ability to generate scientifically productive theories about the causes of sociocultural differences and similarities. Rather than employ concepts that are necessarily real, meaningful, and appropriate from the native point of view, the observer is free to use alien categories and rules derived from the data language of science.[16]

The point is that accurate or objective accounts can be given from either an emic or an etic point of view, but the distinction must be kept clear. If etic pretends to be emic, or emic to be etic, the account becomes confused, troubled, and misleading.

MoMA makes a plain and simple declaration that their approach will be etic. Materials in the press kit which paraphrase a passage of Rubin's introduction argue, "As our focus is on the Modernists' experience of tribal art, and not on ethnological study, we have not included anthropological hypotheses regarding the religious or social purposes that originally surrounded these objects." Rubin similarly argues in his own voice that "the ethnologists' primary concern—the specific function and significance of each of these objects—is irrelevant to my topic, except insofar as these facts might have been known to the modern artists in question."[17] The point of view of Picasso and others, then, is to stand as an etic point of view, and is to be the only focus of MoMA's interest; emic information, such as attributions of motives to the tribal artists, is to be irrelevant.

This position is consistent in itself, but is not consistently acted on. In fact, it is frequently violated. It must be stressed that if the emic/etic question is to

be neglected, then the intentions of the tribal craftsmen must be left neutral and undefined. But Rubin's
argument frequently attributes intentions to the
tribal craftsmen, intentions associated with typically
Modernist esthetic feeling and problem-solving attitudes. The very concept of "affinity" rather than
mere "similarity" attributes to the tribal craftsmen
feelings like those of the Modernist artists, for what
else does the distinction between affinities and acci-
dental similarities mean? The claim that there is an
"affinity of poetic spirit" between Picasso and the
Kwakiutl who made the "sliced" mask attributes to
the Kwakiutl poetic feelings like those of Picasso.
The assertion that their use of "parallelisms and sym-
metries" demonstrates a "propinquity in spirit"[18] between Jacques Lipchitz and a Dogon sculptor attributes to the Dogon a sensibility in general like that
of Lipchitz. And so on. Rubin says that the "specific
function and significance of each of these objects" is
irrelevant—for example, what ceremony the object
was used in, how it was used in the ceremony, and
so on. The use of the word "each" here is tricky. It
is true that Rubin ignores the specific function of
each object, but it is also true that he attributes a
general function to all the objects together, namely,
the esthetic function, the function of giving esthetic
satisfaction. In other words, the function of the
Modernist works is tacitly but constantly attributed
to the primitive works. It is easy to see why no anthropologist was included in the team. Rubin has
made highly inappropriate claims about the intentions of tribal cultures without letting them have

their say, except through the mute presence of their unexplained religious objects, which are misleadingly presented as art objects in the Western sense. This attitude toward primitive objects is so habitual in our culture that one hardly notices the hidden assumptions until they are pointed out. Rubin follows Goldwater in holding that the objects themselves are proof of the formal decisions made, and that the formal decisions made are proof of the esthetic sensibility involved. That this argument seems plausible, even attractive, to us is because we have the same emic view as Rubin and MoMA. But connections based merely on form can lead to skewed perceptions indeed. Consider from the following anthropological example what absurdities one can be led into by assuming that the look of things, without their meaning, is enough to go on:

In New Guinea, in a remote native school taught by a local teacher, I watched a class carefully copy an arithmetic lesson from the blackboard. The teacher had written:
$$4 + 1 = 7$$
$$3 - 5 = 6$$
$$2 + 5 = 9$$
The students copied both his beautifully formed numerals and his errors.[19]

The idea that tribal craftsmen had esthetic problem-solving ambitions comparable to those of Modernist artists attributes to them an evaluation like that which we put on individual creative originality. An anthropologist would warn us away from this presumption: "In preliterate cultures . . . culture is presented to its members as clichés, repeated over and over with only slight variation." "Such art isn't personal. It doesn't reflect the private point of view of an innovator. It's a corporate statement by a group."[20] Yet, again relying only on his sense of the objects, without ethnological support, Rubin declares, "The surviving works themselves attest that individual carvers had far more freedom in varying and developing these types than many commentators have assumed."[21] Surely Rubin knows that the lack of a history of primitive cultures rules out any judgment about how quickly they have changed or how long they took to develop their diversity. The inventiveness Rubin attributes to primitive craftsmen was probably a slow, communal inventiveness, not a matter of individual innovation. In prehistoric traditions, for example, several thousand years may be needed for the degree of innovation and change seen in a single decade of Modernism. Rubin asserts formalist concerns for the tribal craftspeople "even though they had no concept for what such words mean."[22] Consider the particular value judgment underlying the conviction that the only thing primitives were doing that is worth our attention, their proof of "propinquity in spirit" with the white man, was something they weren't even aware of doing.

From a purely academic point of view, Rubin's project would be acceptable if its declared etic stance had been honestly and consistently acted out. What is at issue here, however, is more than a set of academic flaws in an argument, for in other than academic senses the etic stance is unacceptable anyway. Goldwater had made the formalist argument for tribal objects in the '30s; it was a reasonable enough case to make at the time. But why should it be replayed fifty years later, only with more information? The sacrifice of the wholeness of things to the cult of pure form is a dangerous habit of our culture. It amounts to a rejection of the wholeness of life. After fifty years of living with the dynamic relationship between primitive and Modern objects, are we not ready yet to begin to understand the real intentions of the native traditions, to let those silenced cultures speak to us at last? An investigation that really did so would show us immensely more about the possibilities of life that Picasso and others vaguely sensed and were attracted to than does this endless discussion of spiritual propinquity in usages of parallel lines. It would show us more about the "world-historical" importance of the relationship between primitive and Modern and their ability to relate to one another without autistic self-absorption.

The complete omission of dates from the primitive works is perhaps one of the most troubling decisions. Are we looking at works from the '50s? (If so, are they Modern art?) How do we know that some of these artists have not seen works by Picasso? One can foresee a doctoral thesis on Picasso postcards seen by Zairean artists before 1930. The museum dates the Western works, but leaves the primitive works childlike and Edenic in their lack of history. It is true that many of these objects cannot be dated precisely, but even knowing the century would help. I have no doubt that those responsible for this exhibition and book feel that it is a radical act to show how equal the primitives are to us, how civilized, how sensitive, how "inventive." Indeed, both Rubin and Varnedoe passionately declare this. But by their absolute repression of primitive context, meaning, content, and intention (the dates of the works, their functions, their religious or mythological connections, their environments), they have treated the primitives as less than human, less than cultural—as shadows of a culture, their selfhood, their otherness, wrung out of them. All the curators want us to know about these tribal objects is where they came from, what they look like, who owns them, and how they fit the needs of the exhibition.

In their native contexts these objects were invested with feelings of awe and dread, not of esthetic ennoblement. They were seen usually in motion, at night, in closed dark spaces by flickering torchlight. Their viewers were under the influence of ritual, communal identification feelings, and often alcohol or drugs; above all, they were activated by the presence within or among the objects themselves of the shaman, acting out the usually terrifying power represented by the mask or icon. What was at stake for the viewer was not esthetic appreciation but loss of self in identification with and support of the shamanic performance.[23] The Modernist works in the show serve completely different functions, and were made to be perceived from a completely different stance. If you or I were a native tribal artisan or spectator walking through the halls of MoMA we would see an entirely

different show from the one we see as 20th-century
New Yorkers. We would see primarily not form,
but content; not art, but religion or magic.

Consider a reverse example, in which Western cultural objects were systematically assimilated by
primitives into quite a new functional role. In New
Guinea in the '30s, Western food containers were
highly prized as clothing ornaments—a Kellogg's ce-
real box became a hat, a tin can ornamented a belt,
and so on. Passed down to us in photographs, the
practice looks not only absurd but pathetic. We
know that the tribal people have done something so
inappropriate as to be absurd, and without even beginning to realize it. Our sense of the smallness and
quirkiness of their world view encourages our sense
of the larger scope and greater clarity of ours. Yet
the way Westerners have related to the primitive objects that have floated through their consciousness
would look to the tribal peoples much the way their
use of our food containers looks to us: they would
perceive at once that we had done something child-
ishly inappropriate and ignorant, and without even
realizing it. Many primitive groups, when they have
used an object ritually (sometimes only once), desac-
ralize it and discard it as garbage. We then show it
in our museums. In other words, so far are we from
understanding each other that our garbage is their
art, their garbage is our art.

The need to co-opt difference into one's own
dream of order, in which one reigns supreme, is a
tragic failing. Only fear of the Other forces one to
deny its otherness. What we are talking about is a

tribal superstition of Western civilization: the Hegel-based conviction that one's own culture is riding the crucial time-line of history's self-realization. Rubin declares that tribal masterpieces "transcend the particular lives and times of their makers";[24] Varnedoe similarly refers to "the capacity of tribal art to transcend the intentions and conditions that first shaped it."[25] The phrase might be restated: "the capacity of tribal art to be appropriated out of its own intentionality into mine."

As the crowning element of this misappropriation of other values comes the subject of representation. Rubin distinguishes between European canons of representation, which are held to represent by actual objective resemblance, and the various primitive canons of representation, which are held to represent not by resemblance but by ideographic convention. Our representation, in other words, corresponds to external reality, theirs is only in their minds. But the belief that an objective representational system can be defined (and that that system happens to be ours) is naïve and inherently contradictory. It is worth noting that tribal peoples tend to feel that it is they who depict and we who symbolize. Representation involves a beholder and thus has a subjective element. If someone says that A doesn't look like B to him or her, no counterargument can prove that it does. All conventions of representation are acculturated and relative; what a certain culture regards as representation is, for that culture, representation.

Rubin's love of Modernism is based on the fact that it at last took Western art beyond mere illustration. When he says that the tribal artisans are not illustrating but conceptualizing, he evidently feels he is praising them for their modernity. In doing so, however, he altogether undercuts their reality system. By denying that the tribal canons of representation actually represent anything, he is in effect denying that their view of the world is real. By doing them the favor of making them into Modern artists, Rubin cuts reality from under their feet.

The myth of the continuity of Western art history is constructed out of acts of appropriation like those Rubin duplicates. The rediscovery of Greco-Roman works in the Renaissance is an important instance of this, for the way we relate to such art is also in a sense like wearing a cereal-box hat. The charioteer of Delphi, ca. 470 BC, for example, was seen totally differently in classical Greece from the way we now see him. He was not alone in noble, self-sufficient serenity in the room of transcendental angelic whiteness that we see. He was part of what to us would appear a grotesquely large sculptural group—the chariot, the four horses before it, the god Apollo in the chariot box, and whatever other attendants were around. All was painted realistically and must have looked more like a still from a movie than like what we call sculpture. Both Greco-Roman and primitive works, though fragmented and misunderstood, have been appropriated into our art history in order to validate the myth of its continuity and make it seem inevitable.

A belief in the linear continuity of the Western tradition necessitates the claim that Western artists would have come up with primitive-like forms on their own, as a natural development. The purpose of such theorizing is to preclude major breaks in Western art history; its tradition is to remain intact, not pierced and violated by influence from outside the West. The desire to believe in the wholeness, integrity, and independence of the Western tradition has at its root the Hegelian art-historical myth (constructed by the critical historians Karl Schnaase, Alois Riegl, and Heinrich Wölfflin) that Western art history expresses the self-realizing tendency of Universal Spirit. (This is Rubin's vocabulary. He once declared, for example, that Pollock's paintings were " 'world-historical' in the Hegelian sense."[26]) When brought down to earth—that is, to recorded history—this view involves not only the conclusion that the shape and direction of Modern art were not really affected by the discovery of primitive objects, but another conclusion equally unlikely, that the shape and direction of European art were not really influenced by the discovery of Greco-Roman works in the Renaissance.

In fact, Western art history shows three great breaks: one when the population of Europe was changed by the so-called barbarian invasions in the late Roman Empire, which led to the transition from Greco-Roman to Christian art; the second with the Renaissance, the transition from Christian art to European art; the third at the beginning of the 20th century, with the transition from European to Modern art. Each of these breaks in tradition was associated with a deep infusion of foreign influence—

respectively, Germanic, Byzantine, and African/
Oceanic. To minimize these influences is to hold the
Western tradition to be a kind of absolute, isolated
in its purity. In order to support that claim, the adoption of primitive elements by early Modernists is
redefined as a natural, indeed inevitable, inner development of the Western tradition. But the context of
the time suggests otherwise. In the 19th century the
Western tradition in the arts (including literature)
seemed to many to be inwardly exhausted. In 1873
Arthur Rimbaud proclaimed his barbarous Gallic an-
cestors who buttered their hair,[27] and called for a
disorientation of the patterns of sensibility. The feeling was not uncommon; many artists awaited a way
of seeing that would amount simultaneously to an
escape from habit and a discovery of fresh, vitalizing
content. For there is no question that the turn-of-the-
century fascination with archaic and primitive cultures was laden with content: Baudelaire, Rimbaud,
Picasso, and Matisse were attracted, for example, by
the open acknowledgment of the natural status of sex
and death in these cultures. By repressing the aspect
of content, the Other is tamed into mere pretty stuff
to dress us up.

Of course, you can find lots of little things wrong
with any big project if you just feel argumentative.
But I am motivated by the feeling that something
important is at issue here, something deeply, even
tragically wrong. In depressing starkness, *"Primitivism"* lays bare the way our cultural institutions
relate to foreign cultures, revealing it as an ethnocen-
tric subjectivity inflated to co-opt such cultures and

their objects into itself. I am not complaining, as the Zuni Indians have, about having tribal objects in our museums. Nor am I complaining about the performing of valuable and impressive art-historical research on the travels of those objects through ateliers (though I am worried that it buries the real issues in an ocean of information). My real concern is that this exhibition shows Western egotism still as unbridled as in the centuries of colonialism and souvenirism. The Museum pretends to confront the Third World while really co-opting it and using it to consolidate Western notions of quality and feelings of superiority.

Hamish Maxwell, chairman of Philip Morris, one of the sponsors of the exhibition, writes in the catalogue that his company operates in a hundred seventy "countries and territories," suggesting a purview comparable to that of the show. He continues, "We at Philip Morris have benefited from the contemporary art we have acquired and the exhibitions we have sponsored over the past quarter-century. . . . They have stirred creative approaches throughout our company."[28] In the advertisement in the Sunday *New York Times* preceding the *"Primitivism"* opening, the Philip Morris logo is accompanied by the words, "It takes art to make a company great."

Well, it takes more than connoisseurship to make an exhibition great.

NOTES

1. Richard E. Oldenburg, "Foreword," in William Rubin, ed., *"Primitivism" in Twentieth Century Art: Affinity of the Tribal and the Modern*, New York: The Museum of Modern Art, 1984, p. viii.

2. The Museum of Modern Art, New York, press release no.17, August, 1984, for the exhibition *"Primitivism" in Twentieth Century Art: Affinity of the Tribal and the Modern*, p. 1.

3. Revised and republished as Robert Goldwater, *Primitivism in Modern Art*, New York: Vintage Books, 1967. In 1933, 1935, 1941, and 1946, the Modern itself had exhibitions of archaic and primitive objects separately from its Modern collections. René D'Harnancourt, director of the Museum for nineteen years, was an author on the subject.

4. William Rubin, *Dada and Surrealist Art*, New York: Harry N. Abrams, 1965.

5. Two by Rubin, three by Kirk Varnedoe, two by Alan G. Wilkinson, and one each by Ezio Bassani, Christian F. Feest, Jack Flam, Sidney Geist, Donald E. Gordon, Rosalind Krauss, Jean Laude, Gail Levin, Evan Maurer, Jean-Louis Paudrat, Philippe Peltier, and Laura Rosenstock.

6. Presumably, it is this passage that Lynn Cooke refers to as "what Thomas McEvilley . . . calls the primitive with primitivism." I did not actually use that locution. See: "The Resurgence of the Night Mind: Primitive Revivals in Recent Art," in Susan Hiller, ed., *The Myth of Primitivism: Perspectives on Art*, London and New York: Routledge, 1991, p. 141.

7. Varnedoe, "Contemporary Explorations," in Rubin, *"Primitivism,"* pp. 662, 679, 681.

8. Krauss, "Giacometti," in Rubin, *"Primitivism,"* p. 510.

9. Rubin, "Modernist Primitivism: An Introduction," in Rubin, *"Primitivism,"* p. 11.

10. Ibid.

11. Ibid., p. 25.

12. In an article published a year or so after this one appeared, and very much like this one, Hal Foster quotes this phrase ("argument from silence") in quotation marks without attributing it except with the phrase "as others have pointed out." I do not in fact believe that any other author has made this point with this phrase. See: Hal Foster, "The 'Primitive' Unconscious of Modern Art," *October* 34, Fall 1985, p. 49 n.

13. Rubin, "Picasso," in Rubin, *"Primitivism,"* pp. 328–330.

14. Ibid., p. 328.

15. Michelle Wallace, apparently referring to this paragraph, wrote the following, some years after this essay first appeared: "Thomas

McEvilley, [Rubin's] respondent in *Artforum,* would have us shed Western aesthetics for Western anthropology, although, as James Clifford points out in his contribution to the debate, both discourses assume a primitive world in need of preservation, or, in other words, no longer vital and needless to say, incapable of describing itself." See: Michelle Wallace, "Modernism, Postmodernism and the Problem of the Visual in Afro-American Culture," in *Out There: Marginalization and Contemporary Culture,* Russel Ferguson et al., ed., New York: The New Museum of Contemporary Art, and Cambridge, MA: The MIT Press, 1990, p. 47. But the following words, in the same paragraph, seem to have escaped her attention: "No attempt is made [in the *"Primitivism"* exhibition] to recover an emic, or inside, sense of what primitive aesthetics really were or are," where "emic" is glossed with the phrase "the emic viewpoint— that of the tribal participant." I am not, in other words, guilty of her charge that I regard the so-called primitive world as "incapable of describing itself"; on the contrary, that is precisely what I have called for. On pp. 43–44 above I complain that "Rubin has made highly inappropriate claims about the intents of tribal cultures *without letting them have their say. . . .*" (Italics added.) Again, on p. 46 above, one finds: " . . . are we not ready yet . . . to let those silenced cultures speak to us at last?" In fact, not only do I call for tribal accounts of tribal cultures, I call also for their accounts of white Western culture. In the follow-up exchange of letters with Rubin and Varnedoe in *Artforum,* I refer approvingly to Robert Farris Thompson who "has taken Picasso and Amedeo Modigliani reproductions to Africa and recorded the impressions of them given by priests and priestesses of traditional religions of Africa." See the republication of this material in *Discourses: Conversations in Postmodern Art and Culture,* New York: The New Museum of Contemporary Art, and Cambridge, MA: The MIT Press, 1990, p. 388. Wallace, as quoted above, further implies that I "assume a primitive world . . . no longer vital." Perhaps she missed such passages as the following from my side of the dispute: "Roland Kirk plays the didgeridoo in Texas while Mozart's Suzanna sings from a radio in the outback. Today, any artist can be stylistically primitive or stylistically Modern. To perpetuate, on the basis of differences in look, the distinction that obtained a century ago is to commit a blindness worse than that of the eye. There is no longer much justification for the distinction; today, primitive and Modern are elements in a single vocabulary. In the emerging global information moment, classical Yoruba tradition will take its place beside classical Greek tradition, primitivist Modernism beside Modernist primitivism. This is the great and epochal subject that Rubin and Varnedoe so willfully missed." (*Discourses*, p. 394.) One wonders if Wallace has really read this material.

16. Marvin Harris, *Cultural Materialism: The Struggle for a Science of Culture*, New York: Vintage Books, 1980, p. 32.

17. Rubin, "Modernist Primitivism," in Rubin *"Primitivism,"* p. *x*.

18 Ibid., p. 51.

19. Edmund Carpenter, *Oh, What a Blow That Phantom Gave Me!*, New York: Holt, Rinehart and Winston, 1973, p.54.

20. Ibid., pp. 53, 56.

21. Rubin, "Modernist Primitivism," in Rubin, *"Primitivism,"* p. 5.

22. Ibid., p. 19.

23. Sally Price quotes this passage skeptically, without apparent understanding of the context it appears in and without attention to the ethnographic evidence in support of it. See: Sally Price, *Primitive Art in Civilized Places*, Chicago and London: University of Chicago Press, 1989, p. 43. Many ethnographic sources could be cited. Consider, for example, the following passage in Edmund Carpenter's *Oh, What a Blow That Phantom Gave Me!*, New York: Holt, Rinehart and Winston, 1973, p. 22: "I think a great deal of interiors are often dark. Ceremonies outside are frequently held at night by firelight. Costumed performers, which might include just about everyone, are generally masked, with restricted vision, and even when their faces aren't covered, they frequently lower their eyelids, even close their eyes.

"When we put primitive art on museum display, isolated, on a pedestal, against a white background, we violate the intention of the maker and create an effect far removed from the original."

24. Rubin, "Modernist Primitivism," in Rubin, *"Primitivism."*

25. Varnedoe, "Preface," in Rubin, *"Primitivism,"* p. *x*.

26. Cited in Peter Fuller, *Beyond the Crisis in Art*, London: Writers and Readers Publishing Cooperative Ltd., 1980, p. 98.

27. Arthur Rimbaud, *Une Saison en enfer (A season in hell)*, trans. Louise Varèse, New York: New Directions, 1961, p. 7.

28. Hamish Maxwell, in Rubin, *"Primitivism,"* p. *vi*.

For further remarks on some of the themes explored in this article, see the appendices.

Opening the Trap

The Post-Modern Exhibition

A rt's primary social function is to define the communal self, which includes redefining it when the community is changing. Its images, however varied, arcane, or abstract, coalesce in the communal mind into a kind of face hovering in a mirror. The exhibition, in turn, is a ritual attempt to bond a community around a self-definition, whether an established or a new one.[1] From an intimate inspection of the artworks of any culture, it may be inferred what that culture has thought, or has tried to think, of itself at any moment. A museum, as a repository of such moments, is a historically layered picture of the self of a culture. Its permanent collection could be compared to a record on a family wall of the heights of a child at different ages, or a discontinuous series of snapshots of a journey, or time-lapse photography of a river changing its course. Temporary exhibitions also reflect ideas of selfhood, but in fleeting glimpses of the present rather than preserved slices of the past, as the windows that one passes offer glimpses of the minutely changing self upon its way.

Every object implies definitions; but until it is exhibited, its implications lie dormant. It is exhibition that activates this defining power and directs it. The exhibited object has been isolated from the surrounding matrix of things and positioned with deliberation to project a certain assertion of identity onto those who gaze at it. The viewers may, of course, reject the attributions of identity which the exhibited artwork projects, but they must deal with them one way or another, whether through celebratory affirmation, internal resistance, passive acceptance, ironic distancing, or some other stance. The exhibited artwork, then, contains selfhood in a living and formative way as a set of implications and proposals; here something animistic is implied, strangely like the way of speaking about artworks in theories of expression, or about the soul.

An exhibition is a proposition, and usually the proposition is closely focused, since the objects a curator gathers traditionally tend to confirm each other's implications about reality and the role of the self within it. Often there is a layering or series of propositions, emerging as a chain of implications, indeed a whole argument. If the exhibition posits a claim about the quality of the work exhibited, this claim tacitly inverts itself into a definition of quality. At the same time, the assertion about the quality of the exhibited elements unfolds into a third assertion, about their historical importance, and this proposition in turn implies a definition of history. It is the particular flow which will accommodate the particular idea of importance which derives from the particular idea of quality that is embodied in these particular works. Insofar as prevailing ideas of quality, importance, and history determine the sense of human nature and its purpose, the viewer is finally encompassed in a web of propositions which either reinforce or threaten his or her sense of identity and life-meaning. In this sense, the self of the viewer is at stake in an art exhibition, not the self of the artist. The exhibition encroaches on and appropriates the viewer into its mute but focused system of definitions, implications, and propositions.

The appropriation of the viewer is performed not strictly by the artist, who may have been articulating an individual sense of selfhood with no appropriative motives, but by the exhibition organizer or curator, who transposes the artworks from studio to exhibition space, from private to public sphere, positioning or aiming them for their entrapment of the viewer. Museology, in this sense, is the study not of pictures or objects, but of the record of the human self, its trail of definitions and redefinitions, its nakedness in its own past.

In defining the viewer, the exhibited object also makes assertions about the groups to which the viewer belongs. Normally, these assertions confirm a certain class's or clique's belief that its point of view is "natural," at the same time implying that those who are outside such class or clique possess "unnatural" points of view. Superficially, the group elevated to naturalness by the exhibition of a certain definition of quality is elevated as a community of taste; other groups are necessarily understood to lack proper taste. But since in a Platonist milieu (which roughly includes the Kantian esthetics and the formalist criticism derived from it) the "faculty of taste" is a hidden analogue of the soul,[2] the denial of taste amounts to a denial of the humanness of those outside the dominant group. The members of the inner community of taste are also the community of the saved, of those with souls in a world of brutes. Meanwhile, the claim of spiritual superiority masks other claims, including claims to power and, at times, an underlying materialism.[3] One community's hegemony of taste always works to the advantage of some—including those who control its criteria—and to the disadvantage of others—those who see things differently.

In projecting a claim of the naturalness of the values and attitudes of the community for whose bonding rite it was made, an exhibition also implies the universal validity of those values and attitudes and thereby may appear to demonstrate the truth, or at least the hegemony, of the claim. In stable eras, a certain type of exhibition becomes standardized, indicating that society is rigidified round a power structure which regularly validates itself in exhibitions of the fetish objects of the ruling group. By mutual identification with a body of images regarded as its own, the group's interests and its sense of their natural rightness are reinforced. In this way an exhibition is a social event that ritually bonds a class which, though its boundaries may ultimately be economic, is overtly defined through similarity of education and background. It is a more relaxed and less professionally focused bonding rite than the trade convention, but it similarly serves a limited group who know well who they are.

Extreme examples of an art and exhibition style ossified round a stable social structure may be found in ancient Egypt and Medieval Europe—but it is not necessary to look that far afield. Mainstream Modernist art was an array of disguised fetish objects filled with hidden propositions. These propositions functioned as a kind of hidden level of representation which was complexly present in so-called non-representational art. For example, Modernist abstract paintings tended to represent ideas about reality in the way illustrations of metaphysical ideas might do. The visual similarity between the paintings of Piet Mondrian and certain classic styles of 18th-century Indian Tantric abstraction reflects similar metaphysical contents intended by the artists. Both present a metaphorical picture of a mathematical universe ordered from within by a small plurality of eternal forces. Similarly, Jackson Pollock's drip paintings are cosmograms of the idea of metaphysical flux, the process by which entities arise and fall without intermediate periods of fixed definition. Similar observations can be made of much Modernist art, the classical examples of which often had metaphysical intentions.[4] At the same time, these propositions bring with them others about human nature and social reality—that they are metaphysically based and grounded in cosmic laws, and so on.

The artwork's statements about individual identity and metaphysics are conflated into a single dynamic stream in the political dimension, where a type of representing or signifying goes on that unites the individual and the archetypal. Here, the claims and propositions about selfhood are expanded from the individual or the particular interest group to the entire nation. Pre-World-War-II works of the School of Paris, for example, tacitly signify the cultural hegemony of Europe, and especially France, in that period; post-war works of the New York School similarly signify, among other things, the emerging hegemony of America. In embodying the flow of power, the artworks of a dominant culture also validate the claims of a certain way of life; Abstract Expressionist works of the Cold War period, for example, were sent abroad to champion the legitimacy of capitalist democracy over and against communist dictatorship.[5] In a still more expanded and global frame, Modern art as a single massive icon represented the international primacy of the wealthy and educated class who appreciated, collected, and exhibited these Modernist fetishes.

This system of wordless claims generated additional persuasive means as a semantically laden installation style developed around Modernist abstraction. The ostentatiously purified gallery space of the "white cube"[6] makes a claim not only of universality but of eternity. The often windowless, immaculately white exhibition area in which the fetishes of the ruling class are viewed establishes an abstract or idealized non-space, like the ritualized centers of archaic cultures which were understood to be out of ordinary space, time, and causality. The artspace is cut off from any contagion of change, from the movement in the street, from the social divisions and conflicts which are apparent there—such as the confrontation with the homeless—indeed, from the whole context of society as a set of shifting circumstances rather than an eternally sanctioned order. Inside the sheltered gallery or museum, as in a space consecrated for religious rites, there is a communion of wine and bread on the opening night. After that, consumption, which is a sign of change and process, is forbidden; the visitors do not eat, drink, sleep, or laugh there. The bathrooms are hidden so as to negate the defecation process with its *sic transit* message. The only consumption allowed, that of buying the artworks, goes on in secret behind closed doors. Like the ancient ritual center—the space atop the ziggurat or inside the pyramid—the artspace is an umbilicus leading to eternity; through it, the ratification of eternity is cast upon certain objects and, by extension, upon the attitudes and hegemony of the class to whom they belong. The quasi-eternal look of the setting implies that the ratification of these works will never lose force or change; accordingly, the taste (soul) behind the works is projected unto eternity, as, in effect, divinely sanctioned or ordained; the social structure based upon that taste is, through the sympathetic magic of eternalizing its fetishes, similarly distanced from the idea of change.[7] The exhibition style thus contributes further hidden propositions to the network of persuasions.

When one culture exhibits the objects of another, the set of propositions and appropriations is expanded still further. From the scale of the individual, the interest group, the nation, and the international class, the exhibition now focuses relations among multinational culture groups. The primary case in point, of course, is the exhibition by Western colonialist cultures of the objects of so-called Third World, or colonized, cultures. In this situation the exhibited objects, often religious fetishes in their original contexts, become fetishes of the secular religion of imperialism, justifying it symbolically by their forced submission to it. As early as the 17th century, the idea was common in Europe that colonial conquests had demonstrated the superiority of Western civilization. This view was reinforced in 19th-century curio rooms and early ethnographic museums, where "captured" tribal objects represented Modernist Western culture's conquest of traditional societies, much as booty brought home from dark-skinned peoples was displayed in the triumphal processions of ancient Rome. The booty of colonialism is also its validation, proof of its superiority. Like the *templum Augusti* in the far reaches of the Roman Empire, such as Barygaza in India, the captured objects represent the long arm of Western civilization reaching around the world, taking what it wants, and willing to fight for its right to do so.[8]

Captured tribal objects came to be called art by Western commentators in the early 20th century and began to be shifted from ethnological to art museums, being appropriated ever more deeply into the array of Modernist fetishes asserting Western superiority. The colonizer's reinterpretation of these objects away from their makers' intentions—foisting

its will onto the intentionality of a foreign will—
represents a continuing invasion of the integrity of
the foreign culture. It assumes that the makers of the
objects did not understand their own intentions, that
it took the allegedly superior gaze of the Western
connoisseur to tell them what their objects really
were for. Transported now from ethnological to art
museums, the appropriated objects mutely yet elo-
quently embody the claim that the transcendent gaze
of Western culture sets right the misunderstandings
of other peoples around the globe.[9]

Modernist exhibition strategy holds that the installation of tribal objects in the purified art gallery setting frees them from context in order to open them
to appreciation as pure art; in fact, it puts them in the
context of Western claims to be above context. It
colonizes them again, in retrospect, in a delectation
of their corpses. The esthetic or formalist idea of art
is enforced upon objects of other primary intentions.
The Hegelian historicist view is forced upon objects
conceived in a different feeling toward time. Western
criteria of quality are forced upon works that, even
as art, were not made with the West in mind. The
result is a global claim for the universality of a certain
idea of quality, or a certain taste.

The belief that there were universal and unchanging values and that these values resided in the cultural
and social policies of Western Europe and America
—essentially, of the colonizing nations—was characteristic of Modernism, indeed, one of its historical
premises. Hegelian Modernism posited history as a
teleological force which was working toward a goal;

this force, a subjective universal working through objective particulars, had to receive definition and leadership from a group of hyper-conscious individuals who would, through superior vision or intuition, see the values toward which history was inwardly striving and help it on its way. This role was assumed by the colonialist nations, much as the Crusaders had once justified conquest as the saving of souls.

Modernism, relying on a mysticism of progress and scientific method, saw itself as a global or transcendent viewpoint capable of standing above and judging the countless tribal points of view. Lately, it has come to seem a tribal view itself, that of Western Christendom since the Renaissance. The uncriticized self-image of Western Christendom has involved the role of conquerer since at least the Crusades. Perhaps as a result, the contact with other cultures which the Crusades began and colonialism intensified did not at once suffice to relativize European (or Christian) attitudes on a broad scale, but, through enforced submission, seemed to reinforce them. More recently, the sense of the community of nations as a global village has caused Western attitudes to be criticized and relativized from within. The threat of Western culture to destroy the ecosystem of the entire earth, if not to blow the earth itself to Kingdom Come, the ravaging of southeast Asia through neo-colonial interferences, the long stalemate of the Cold War—all this and more brought into awareness the fact that Western culture, seen historically, could not be unlimitedly validated by mere symbolism anymore. The mindless conviction of its universality and eternality was shaken. Consequent social upheavals have resonated through the world of art.

The sense that one's culture is not a standard by which all others are to be measured, but merely one stance among many, is the essence of the reversal of will that is called post-Modernism, which relativizes all communities of taste. This does not mean the end of quality, or of the authority of taste, but its limitation to a conditioned group. Within a community of similarly conditioned people, consensual standards of quality define and bond and are, within the limits of that consensus, valid. Within another community, however, or within the same community at another time, completely different standards may obtain, equally real at their moment, and real in precisely the same way: that they offer their group a field for self-reflection and self-definition, a mirror in which to glimpse the meanings of its changes and developments, as well as its relatively unchanging foundational assumptions.

A post-Modern exhibition strategy begins with the realization that categories and criteria have no innate validity—only the validity that is projected upon them—and thus that their transgression can be an opening into freedom. In terms of the culture of the exhibition, this means that humans can exhibit anything whatever to one another for whatever reasons. The post-Modern exhibition does not compete in the conflict of different ideas of quality, priority, or historical centrality. It allows different intentions, definitions, and standards of quality to stand side by side without giving one of them dominance or authority over the others. Similarly, the post-Modern agenda of art history calls for studies of the relativity of canons, both from one age to another within the same tradition and from one tradition to another. The point of such studies will not be the search for an essence common to all, but a stress upon difference itself.

The post-Modern exhibition must strive not for slices of sameness, as in the Modernist exhibition with its attempt to universalize a canon, but for a focus on difference which honors the Other and allows it to be itself, without trying to reduce all difference by the authoritarian postulation of a hidden sameness. It involves the difficult ideal of letting things be what they are, or what they were when they were themselves, before being appropriated into categories not their own. Failing this, it involves at least an awareness, or an attempt at awareness, of the category- and quality-projections involved, their motives and limitations. It posits no unifying idea of quality, but many pluralistic and relativized ideas of it; no unifying idea of the mainstream, no unifying idea of art history or indeed of history, no clarified hierarchy. In the '80s, the relativization of Western attitudes led to a new approach to non-Western cultures with a fascinated sense of the reality of their otherness not as a noble-savage romanticism but as a shared, indeed mutually dependent, interest in the future.

Magicians of the Earth[10] is a landmark attempt to

implement a post-Modern exhibition strategy—meaning a strategy that consciously attempts to neglect the Modernist beliefs in universal canons, in the Eurocentric view of history governed by progress, and in the transcendent reality of pure form. Writing before the exhibition, I do not know (nor may I, perhaps, after) how well *Magicians of the Earth* will fulfill its post-Modern agenda. But the importance of that agenda strikes me as beyond question. *Magicians* hopes to provide a sense of the global state of contemporary art with all its fragmentations and differences. The reality of contemporary art as a shared enterprise of artists in Europe, America, India, China, Japan, Australia, Egypt, and so on requires a revised view of history as having multiple streams and multiple directions. Contemporary artists in India assimilate the Schools of Paris and New York as European and American artists once assimilated something of the art of Africa and Oceania. Contemporary artists in China struggle to interweave traditional styles a thousand years old and influences that are currently entering from the West. Contemporary Australian aboriginal artists find overlaps between their traditional styles and 1960's abstraction. Contemporary artists in Greece turn their eyes from the Akropolis to the work of Joseph Beuys and back again.

The inner contradiction of the project is that there is no defining without that which is outside the definition, and no bonding of a group without an Other in distinction to which it bonds. Seeking not to impose categories but to create an openness, *Magi-*

cians defines the indefinite, or the contradictory manifold, and proposes a bonding around contradiction, plurality, and lack of essence, around an idea of the self as relative, multi-faceted, and shifting. The difficulty of this project is proportional to its importance. Its central problem, perhaps, will be to handle the quasi-universal scale of the exhibition without a positing of universals, to avoid the Platonic affirmations of universal and eternal validity which may arise from an ecstatic sense of global bonding.

NOTES

1. See Thomas McEvilley, "On the Art Exhibition in History: The Carnegie International and the Redefinition of the American Self," in exhibition catalogue, *Carnegie International*, Pittsburgh: The Carnegie Museum of Art, 1988, pp. 18–23.

2. Kant's idea of the faculty of judgment, or taste, goes back in the history of thought to Plato's "eye of the soul" described in the *Republic* (7.527e, 533d). Plotinus' form of the doctrine (*Enneads* 5.8.1) became the basis for 18th- and 19th-century esthetic theory from Shaftesbury to Kant to Goethe.

3. This is exemplified by Bernard Berenson's collaboration with the dealer Joe Duveen, who offered him 25% of sales on works which Berenson would misrepresent to clients, using his authoritarian position in the world of taste—his priestlike credential of soul—to engineer his own advantage. (See Colin Simpson, "The Bilking of Jules Bache," *Connoisseur*, October, 1986, and "The Berenson Scandal," ibid.) Clement Greenberg's profiteering off of sales of works by artists whom he had used the authority of his dictatorship of taste to elevate and validate is a similar example.

4. For a group of essays on this aspect of Modern art see Maurice Tuchman, *The Spiritual in Art: Abstract Painting 1890–1985*, New York: Abbeville Press, 1986. Also, Thomas McEvilley, "The Opposite of Emptiness," in *Artforum* March, 1987, and "Heads It's Form, Tails It's Not Content," in *Art & Discontent*, Kingston, NY: Documentext/McPherson & Co., 1991, pp. 23–58.

5. See the materials gathered in Francis Frascina, ed., *Pollock and After, The Critical Debate,* New York: Harper and Row, 1985.

6. As Brian O'Doherty called the post-Betty Parsons style of exhibiting Modern art. See O'Doherty, *Inside the White Cube: The Ideology of the Gallery Space,* introduction by Thomas McEvilley, Santa Monica, CA: Lapis Press, 1986.

7. Since the criteria of quality which underlie the works will supposedly never change, the artworks incorporating them become transcendent investment objects, more stable than currency or stocks, out of reach of socially induced fluctuations in value. This process was concretized, or made into an objective correlative, when the New York stock market crashed on October 19, 1987, and the world market trembled; as stocks plummeted, the value of artworks went up. Art was transcendently legitimized as incorporating values more profound and durable than the values of money and of material reality in general. Art's traditional connection with religion, and hence with the idea of a type of value "beyond" the material, is secretively invoked in this market context, as it was in the criticism which emphasized pure form.

8. For the *templum Augusti* in Barygaza, see Sir Mortimer Wheeler, *Rome Beyond the Imperial Frontiers,* London: Bell, 1954, p. 177.

9. A recent particularly notorious instance of such misappropriation was the Museum of Modern Art's 1984 show, *"Primitivism" in Twentieth Century Art.* Leashed as appendages to the history of modern Western art, the appropriated objects, from Africa, Oceania, and elsewhere, were not only wrested out of their native intentionalities and value-systems, but were subordinated to objects which in fact had derived from them, to which, in an inversion of historical sequence, they were invoked as footnotes. The tribal objects were dragged into a view of history to which they had not contributed, a view which consisted in part in their subordination. The bonding function of the exhibition was carried to a perverse extremity here. By identifying superficially and misguidedly with objects from non-Western cultures, the Western audience wrested them out of their identity group without genuinely including them in another, leaving them adrift with little mooring on a sea of unpredictable and explosive changes of meaning.

10. This essay, the "keynote statement" of the exhibition catalogue, was written of course before the exhibition took place; some of my thoughts and feelings about the exhibition after it had taken place appear in Appendix A.

Exhibitions, Real and Imaginary

R *eal Exhibition:* In a small city in central China, when I asked to visit the local museum, two minibuses of Chinese took on the job of escorting me: an interpreter, a driver, a security man, a liaison with foreign ministry, a liaison with local institutions, a second driver, a second interpreter, a second security man, two arrangers of meals, and myself. Our caravan pulled into the barren and ripped-up yard of the museum, which seemed closed, and waited for the director. He arrived in a Western business suit and, after trying to dissuade us from seeing the museum at all, reluctantly unlocked a door to a small back room. We gazed in silence on a few potsherds lying on dusty shelves. Aside from these, he said, the entire collection had been removed to Beijing while work was done on the building. Work had long since stopped. The collection, whatever it was, might not be returned, he feared, in his lifetime.

★ ★ ★

The Witoto, a tribe of about a thousand people in the Amazon basin of Colombia, call themselves "the

73

people of the center of the world," and distinguish themselves from other groups, whom they call "the people of the animals." When such isolated tribal groups are raided, colonized, enslaved, or amalgamated into national states, they undergo a shock of non-recognition which relativizes their own sense of things by revealing the existence of others. No longer at the center, they may seem to have been abandoned by their gods and erased from the map of reality.

★ ★ ★

A fully equipped scholar's library in 12th-century Europe would have contained about one hundred books. *Imaginary Exhibition:* A shelf about four feet long containing modern editions of these works: this was the universe, then.

★ ★ ★

When a tribal point of view is breaking down, subgroups may arise which re-create, on a smaller scale, the sense of oneness and centrality that characterized the lost childhood stage of the tribe. Initiation cults fulfill this purpose, from the Buddhist *sangha* at the time of the formation of the Magadha state in Northern India, to the Pythagorean brotherhood at the time of the spread of Hellenic statehood, to the Freemasons or Rosicrucians at the time of the formation of national states in late Renaissance Europe, to the cult of the Dreamer among 19th-century Amerindians, who, in the face of the demolition of their tradition, were told to seek the real world in sleep.

★ ★ ★

Real Exhibition: Herodotus says that Babylonian priests would gather once a year before dawn to watch the sunrise reach a certain pillar deep within the temple; as the sun touched the horizon, a gem inlaid in the pillar would glow for a few moments, indicating that the world still worked.

★ ★ ★

The community of Modern art, especially of Modernist abstraction, was in part a cultic attempt to regain a sense of wholeness and unity that the society around no longer provided with sufficient intensity. The ritual practice of the exhibition functioned like the worship of relics or sacramental substances. It ratified a certain community of taste, and with it, at a somewhat hidden level, a community of shared spiritual and social ambitions.

★ ★ ★

Real Exhibition: In the initiation into the Eleusinian mysteries, the hierophant, or exhibitor of the sacred things, would take certain objects from a basket and silently display them to the initiands in the midst of a great light: these may have included a golden ear of wheat, a snake, clay models of male and female genitals, and so on. Plato says that the chamber would fill with ghostly apparitions, and Pausanias records that someone who intruded upon the ceremony died soon, a story designed, of course, to keep intruders out. In the Modernist exhibition, the elite community of taste serves the same purpose: the art-works speak only to the initiates, keeping their secrets safe from interlopers.

★   ★   ★

In ancient Pythagorean circles, there were dancers who could expound the Pythagorean doctrines completely and in detail through coded movements. *Imaginary Exhibition:* A dance which means nothing to the audience, but which is completely coded for the performer, is followed by a dance which is coded for the audience but not for the performer, who has simply learned the movements.

★   ★   ★

Modernism involved a cultic belief in progress and a messianic belief in a Western avant garde which would make it happen. Hidden in the myth was a vestigial form of the restoration of Eden. The idea that the nations of Europe were the leaders of history and that the colonized peoples lacked souls parallels the Witoto belief that they were at the center of the world and other people were "of the animals." But, unlike the enslaved Witoto, the nations of Europe managed for a while to enforce this view on others.

★   ★   ★

In ancient Sumer, when a temple was being built, the whole city would observe a ritual silence, in case something inauspicious might be said and overheard by the gods. The prerequisite of silence, or of low-level speech, which prevails in modern art museums, is covertly posited on similar assumptions about sacredness and the attentiveness of higher powers.

★   ★   ★

At present, Western culture, while it feels—or hopes—it has seen the end of Modernism, has not gotten beyond the transitional point of calling its situation post-Modern. Post-Modernism is defined primarily not as itself (for it has not yet really revealed itself) but by its renunciation of Modernist beliefs in progress, hierarchy, and the center. Post-Modernism means the piercing, at last, of the tribal bubble in which European Modernism, like the Witoto, saw itself as the human center of a world not otherwise endowed with humanness—a world which, in effect, begged to be conquered and guided.

★   ★   ★

Imaginary Exhibition: World maps from different times and places and with different projection systems are exhibited in various patterns which confute one another, chronology offset by political geography, reoriented by formal resemblances, geological history, poetic associations. Behind the boundaries of maps lies the hidden blood of wars, as tribal realities confront and conflate with one another.

★   ★   ★

Where Modernism was absolutistic, post-Modernism might be relativistic. Where Modernism was based on hierarchies, post-Modernism might work to level the hierarchies and see what is left that can serve as a direction. Where Modernism was universalist in its championing of a certain idea of quality, post-Modernism might recognize the appropriateness of different ideas of quality to different cultural situations. Whereas Modernism believed that history proper was an activity only of white people living in Europe (and lately America), post-Modernism might open up history to the Third World—or find that this has already been done without anyone asking permission.

★ ★ ★

Western visitors to the Anglo-Egyptian Book Shop in Cairo, Egypt, are confronted with shelves of books on subjects that will not be seen in Western bookshops—*The History of Zambia, The History of Indonesia, The History of the New Hebrides,* and so on. These histories tend to start in the 19th or 20th centuries.

★ ★ ★

Imaginary Exhibition: What India came to see as a second or "enlightenment" brain atop the Buddha's head was a hairstyle in 4th-century-BC Greece. Indian sculptors took the image from Greeks in Gandhara and moved it in one direction; Cambodian sculptors took it in another, Nepalese, Tibetan, Chinese, Japanese, Burmese, Ceylonese, in yet others. Each version implied a somewhat altered proposal about human nature and the world it confronts.

★ ★ ★

The concept of an "imaginary exhibition" suggests
an imaginary humanness; it offers an open space in
which proposals about humanness can be made. An
exhibition which makes a radically new proposal
about the meaning of human life is experienced as
shocking and difficult, albeit sometimes compelling,
sometimes even liberating.

★ ★ ★

Real Exhibition: The *Houston Post,* Feb. 2, 1989:
"Authorities closed China's first major avant garde
art exhibition in many years after unruly young artists broke a ban on performances of action art at its
opening, organizers said Monday. 'People are just
not ready for this kind of art,' said critic Fei Dawei
outside the China Art Gallery in Beijing.... The
exhibition of more than 300 pieces by 130 artists
opened with a burst of 'spontaneous art happenings'
Sunday. One artist washed his feet in bowls of
water, another sold live shrimp, some threw money
and condoms onto the ground. Police evacuated
spectators from the vast gallery in central Beijing and
closed down the exhibition."

★ ★ ★

In an era of a stable status quo, the prevalent exhibition style reinforces the prevalent definition of things
and re-imprints it on the viewers. When a culture is
shaken and its definitions are coming apart, the exhibition can reinforce the crumbling definitions or it

can begin the redefining, contributing to the flow of change an image which might be a hint of the future.

★   ★   ★

Chinese art schools started using nude models (only female) in 1984. Visitors to the schools have noticed that the students, both male and female, represent women in their pictures with whiter skin and larger breasts than the Chinese models who are seated before them have.

★   ★   ★

At the present moment, useful exhibition strategies might stress: the difference between a culture's idea of itself at one moment and its idea of itself at the next; the difference between one culture's use of a sign and another culture's adaptation of it to new purposes; the differences between canons of quality; the search for an array of objects that are irremediably different from one another, an array about which one could think of nothing to say.

★   ★   ★

The New York Times Service, Beijing, Dec, 20, 1988: "A mix of curiosity and prurience drew record crowds of 10,000 a day for 18 straight days to the Beijing Art Gallery [for China's first show of nude art]. . . . 'Oh, I'm so embarrassed,' stammered Chen Hong, a medical student, when asked why she came to see the exhibition. Miss Chen blushed and hid her face with her hands while hastily adding: 'This is the first time I've seen this kind of thing.' . . . Each visitor paid the equivalent of 60 cents admission, 10 times the normal ticket price in China and equivalent to a half-day's wages.... Some stood gaping at the most realistic and sensuous of the paintings; others hurried by in horror...."

The post-Modern exhibition might bring together objects that would compromise one another's claims to quality and essence, each contradicting or at least casting a shadow of irony over the other, rendering it naïve in its simplicity. Such an exhibition would present itself by contradicting itself at every turn.

The New York Times, Dec. 26, 1988, Phnom Penh: "The Tuol Sleng Museum of Genocidal Crime is a part of the standard itinerary of visitors [to Cambodia].... There is ... a map of Cambodia made of human skulls, with the Tonle Sap Lake and its rivers red, of course, with blood.... Workers on a break chat in the shade next to mounds of skulls. Reed baskets and water jars are stuffed with femurs. Thigh bones lie bleaching on a bamboo pallet in the sun.... [Back] at the National Museum in Phnom Penh a guide [extols] ... the extraordinary collection of Khmer art...."

The confrontation with difference—with, implicitly, the Other—will not be easy. Both the curatorial heroism and the curatorial formalism of the post-

Modern exhibition could arise in this struggle—the former in the effort to keep its articulation of difference from masking a claim for a longed-for sameness, and the latter in what will emerge as its exquisite attempt to articulate difference with a precision that is almost a preciosity.

★ ★ ★

Before an Egyptian priest entered the temple, he would shave his body entirely from head to foot. The precaution was not about cleanliness, but the intense symbolic importance of defining one group and keeping others out: not only uninitiated humans, but even the profane eyes of fleas or ticks or other vermin that live in the body hair must not be allowed to see the rites and icons.

★ ★ ★

With this extremity of precaution, Egyptian culture endured for centuries without noticeable change. Is it possible anymore to keep things out?

★ ★ ★

A post-Modern exhibition might avoid the absolutism of both presence (essence) and absence (emptiness). It might remain in the corrupt (and fertile) zone of intersection, mediation, and cross-pollution.

★ ★ ★

Traditionally, a Buddhist monk would contemplate a human corpse in the process of decay, sitting beside it all day and all night every day and every night until the process was over. Through traditional meditation practices, he would transpose the activity imaginatively into his own body, his own hopes and ambitions. *Imaginary Exhibition:* A corpse is displayed in a vitrine until the visible process of decay is over. (Can a culture criticize its own ambition for eternal life?)

★ ★ ★

In 1985, visiting a guru in the Himalayas whom I had visited fifteen years earlier, I found bulldozers eating away the back of the hill in which he lived in a kind of large burrow. I asked him if he knew the highway was coming, and he laughed and said, "That's all a dream, a dream." A quarter of a mile away you could hear them tearing through the hill.

★ ★ ★

The New York Times: Beijing, Feb. 8, 1989: "The police released an artist today after holding her for three days for shooting a BB gun at her own sculpture in an exhibition of avant-garde art."

The Selfhood of the Other

Reflections of a Westerner on the Occasion of an Exhibition of Contemporary Art from Africa

Plato says somewhere that if you're shipwrecked and washed up on a beach, and you see drawings in the sand showing that people have been studying geometry, you know you're all right: you've landed in civilization.

Carl Trahman, Classics professor, remarked in 1966: If you go somewhere to give a talk, and you sit down to dinner and see that they've put marshmallows in the salad, you know at last you've arrived in the realm of the Other.

Modernism. At the heart of Modernism was a myth of history designed to justify colonialism through an idea of progress. The West, as self-appointed vanguard, was to lead the rest of the world, forcefully if necessary, toward a hypothetical utopian future—a great deal of wealth changing hands along the way.[1] The passing of Modernism, then, means the passing of the mentality of the colonial era, and especially of the view of history that was its cover story. "Post-Modern," "post-historical," and "post-colonialist," therefore, are more or less synonymous terms.

In the discourse about contemporary art, "post-Modern" is often used to describe certain formal developments and esthetic shifts, without reference to the larger sphere of political, social, and economic history. But the view of art history that is passing, with its teleological emphasis on linear sequences of formal change, was merely an aspect of the Modernist myth which justified colonialism. Stated very briefly: Modern art, with its imperative of formal evolution—and above all, abstract art, with the claim that it transcended social forces—was an emblem of the master-soul of Euro-Modernism; it provided an exemplary array of evolution-like developments that were taken to guarantee that history was indeed engaged, under Western leadership, in an adventure of progress.

Post-Modernism in the visual arts is part of the global project of cultural decolonization. It involves (among other things) an attempt on the part of Western people to get beyond strictly European ideas of esthetics and its history—ideas heretofore integral to their sense of identity. The project has many dangers, among them what Kumkum Sangari has referred to as "an institutionalized 'third-worldism' . . . [that makes] an attempt to re-annex the colonial subject . . . through the application of recent de-essentializing critical theories pitted against bourgeois, colonial, Enlightenment value systems."[2]

Objects. In the colonial period, objects made by non-Western cultures were brought back to the West not only as booty but as evidence. They were understood, at however mute a level, as proof of the superiority of the colonialists—that was the point of calling the colonized cultures "primitive." How their objects were treated upon arrival reflected the shifting valuation of the Other in the West.

First, the colonized peoples were regarded as somehow less than human. In terms of the discourse prevalent in 16th-century Christendom, the Conquistadors, encountering the native peoples of the New World, regarded them as not possessing souls—that is, as not participating in the advance of Providence and in the Christian eschatology of death, judgment, Heaven, and Hell. They were creatures on the level of, say, parrots, who could be eaten, kept as pets, taught languages which they did not understand, or plucked for their feathers. This mode of dealing with other cultures is very ancient. Aristotle suggested that the Scythians were not human, though they looked like humans. African groups commonly thought the first white colonizers were not human either. The European colonial myth of the non-humanness of conquered peoples was evident in the claim that those people were outside of history—history being the white way of organizing the narrative of communal memory. Their ahistoricity in turn was demonstrated by, among other things, their supposedly unchanging art—its eternal or Edenic stasis negating the dynamic onrush of events among historical peoples.[3] Examples of this preternatural art that found their way to the West were kept alongside elephant tusks or peacock's feathers in "curio rooms." They were parts of nature, not of culture; the project of colonization would supposedly shift them from the former category to the latter.

Later in the colonial process, the conquered peoples gradually came to be seen as human after all. At this point, their art began to have a double significance in Western ways of dealing. On the one hand, these things now seemed to be art, the emblem of the soul, and thus to indicate the humanity of their makers. On the other hand, this art was still perceived as ahistorical, demonstrating that colonial cultures, to be brought into history, still needed to be under the wing of Western tutors. Now the objects were transported from curio rooms to museums, at first ethnographic museums, then art museums.

At about this stage of the process—the early years of the 20th century—*our* (meaning white Western) artists started making objects like *their* (meaning non-white, non-Western) artists. These objects, in fact, were the basis of what we call Modern art.[4] That passage of influence reflected an alteration in our habit (it was not non-human models we were miming), but not a sufficiently large one to make "them" seem Modern in "our" regard. For that, another reversal was needed: the moment when colonialized peoples started making objects like ours would indicate that they had been drawn into history—that they had Orphically remembered the true meaning of their identity as human. At that moment the West would begin to call their art "contemporary," a term that does not apply to ahistorical or timeless things, and which previously had been accorded primarily to objects made in Paris or New York.

Geometry or Marshmallows? When one culture regards the objects of another, those objects are instantly incorporated into an alien mental framework; they are helplessly interpreted through some habit of thought different from the habit of their makers. That this should be regarded as a negative outcome, as a rape of the object or as a violation of its essence, implies that an artifact, as a thing made by a human, is as ethnically particular as its human maker, and that its ethnicity is contained in it like a kind of soul. The system of thought of the maker is felt to be alertly present in the object in such a way that the object is abused by regarding it through some other system of thought. (Here fetishism and the Expression Theory of art merge.[5])

Similarly, to see an object in another place than that in which and for which it was made is to see it surrounded with questions: How and why did it get to that new place? Was it stolen by some imperial force? Is its itinerary a record of economic exploitation or violent abuse? The Zuni and some other non-European peoples have sought the return of their objects from Western museums of art and ethnography, on the grounds that the objects contain specific powers that are perturbed by placing them in an alien cultural environment. The government of Greece has long sought the return of the Elgin Marbles from the British Museum, implying that objects are tied to the places of their facture. Yet it is unlikely that a Western European country would seek the return of, say, Old Master paintings from Japan or elsewhere in the non-Western world. Power relationships govern these (as other) feelings. The dissemination of Western cultural objects into non-Western cultures is seen as an assertion of Western power and influence, a kind of proselityzing mission. But the confinement of non-Western objects in Western museums is seen in quite an opposite way, as a sign of the bondage of this other culture to Western power, of the appropriation of its wealth and indeed its identity by an alien force.

"The Animals." In its ideal state, an emic, or culturally inherited, world view might be that of a cultural group which has no knowledge whatever of other cultural groups and which believes that its own styles of cognition are all that exist—that they are, in effect, the natural and absolute ways of being. The Witoto have traditionally referred to themselves as "the People of the Center of the World" and to other groups as "the People of the Animals"—a distinction parallel to the European distinction between culture and nature.[6] Any group which has not relativized its own inherited attitudes by acknowledging the claims of other groups' attitudes is emic. Into such a setting comes the Western anthropologist. Like an Olympian viewing many warring groups from on high, he is aware that there are various approaches to the meanings of things, and he sees the Witoto approach as just one among many. His approach is called etic, meaning that it transcends the level of the emic by a cognitive meta-step.[7]

Western science is widely regarded as constituting the strongest claim at present to an etic position—presumably because of its proven effectiveness at intervening in nature, but perhaps also because of a residual persuasiveness in the Modernist myth. This claim of science exerts strong appeal in what Badri Raina has called the "transnational *countryside*"[8] of the Third World. It is expressed, for example, in Sangari's dread of reversion to the emic: "The question which insistently arises . . . is that if we refuse to grant total interpretative value to linear, western, cognitive modes, then what options do we have apart from reactive indigenisms."[9] But the elevation of the Western scientist to the role of transcendent arbiter seems, possibly, to be only another emic approach, perhaps projected outward as unself-critically as the world view of the Witoto. The record of anthropological accounts often shows an entrenched complacency of cultural attitude not altogether different from the Conquistadors'. A more genuinely etic attitude might emerge if the scientist had relativized his own position as well. (But would that be an attitude or a non-attitude?)

Soul-Vendors. To an etic culture, it seems reasonable, even normal, to make goods destined for sale in foreign markets. But to a traditional emic mentality there may be something shocking about making goods for cultures other than one's own. There is

indeed something almost impossible about it, because it involves making objects that one does not
understand—an alienation of one's labor from one's
soul. (My red-and-black-checked flannel jacket with
the label "Lumberjack" inside the collar was made
in Bangladesh.) Is it one's intention, one's power—
one's soul, as it were—that one sends overseas for
alien exchange? Does this represent a willful sellout
by the native maker to a foreign power? Or an ambiguous confusion and merging of selves/others into
some new and possibly horrible entity?

In his introduction to Franz Fanon's *The Wretched
of the Earth,* Jean-Paul Sartre wrote of the first members of a conquered culture to adopt the ways of the
conquerors. He saw them as essentially lost beings,
who have sold their souls and those of their natural
fellows and in consequence have become blanks,
soulless, neither one thing nor another. They have
betrayed the whole project of identity. But this feeling seems to assume the integrity of the colonized
individual before the colonialist overlay has affected
his or her livelihood and, hence, personality. It seems
a wishful Edenic myth of cultural purity to believe
that humans were once psychologically and socially
whole, and that it is the mixing of cultures which
destroys this wholeness and creates monsters. Does
this then mean that culture-mixing is impossible, or
inevitably destructive, and that it can never produce
healthy results? There is something misbegotten and
puritanical here, like an insistence on ethnic purity.

Sartre's detestation for the colonized servant's betrayal of his or her tradition implies that all cultural

influence from outside should be rejected or resisted. The popular 1980 movie *The Gods Must Be Crazy* shows a situation in which a Coca-Cola bottle (representing "Coca-colonization," or cultural neo-colonialism) is rejected from an African community the way a living body may reject a surgical implant. The motif relates to the utopian and puritanical idea of returning all objects to their original places. It represents a desire to freeze the world, and to prevent all change in it—ultimately a desire to maintain the emic point of view forever.

This attitude assumes something like the Hegelian idea that each culture has a nature or essence. In the metaphysical puritanism of Modernism, to compromise a thing's essence seemed perhaps worse than to destroy the thing outright: it is to make it into something which annihilates it ideologically while simultaneously taking over its being. The intrusive force activates the thing's survival in such a way as to betray it at every moment it survives. Its existence is based on a continuing betrayal of its reason for existing. The desire to return objects to their places of origin implies that an artifact has an essence that reflects its maker's ethnicity. Since essences do not change, any significant culture-mixing is impossible or, even worse, hideous.

Monster Mash. The individual whom Sartre denounces is in fact a kind of monster, in the Greek mythological sense of a being with the traits of two or more species at once: a human collage, or pastiche. The point that Sartre may have missed, viewing these things from the heart of late Modernism, is that the process of change works through such monstrosity; a being containing part of one era and part of another at the same time is a being moving into the future, like Zeno's arrow occupying two places at once in its flight. Cultural change occurs through the interposition of pastiche, and the ontology of monstrosity, collage, and pastiche is absolutely characteristic of the post-Modern or post-colonial project. Western artworks by Picasso incorporating elements of African or Oceanic art are pastiche monsters; Indian artworks by Tyeb Mehta employ elements of Matisse, and African artworks by Iba N'Diaye engage School-of-Paris painterliness. The fecundity of these new hybrid species offers a cross-fertilization from which a challenging future might grow.

The Siren Song. An infrequently asked question is why one culture would want the objects of another in the first place. In some cases, of course, the imported objects may be more efficient for a practical purpose—say, the advantages of iron over bronze. Otherwise, a conqueror may wish to display booty as signs of conquest, or a colonial may see the objects of the ruling class as status symbols. Sometimes the desire for alien objects comes because people are sick of their own culture and want a hole through its shell into an outside. In these cases, the desire for contact with an alien culture is a desire for an exotic otherness that one feels as a new component of identity. To the disaffiliated member of a culture, possessing the alien object is like a talisman of promised freedom, like possessing another soul, or a channel to one (somewhat as the Latin poet Ennius remarked that he had three souls because he spoke three languages). Through appreciating objects from an alien culture, one may discover the relativity of one's own inherited tastes. In an emic situation, it is natural to think that one's taste is inborn and universal. Only after etic relativizations does it become clear that taste is not inborn, because judgments of quality change.

Thus, the dialogue that takes place when goods travel back and forth is complex. At first, it is often a dialogue of exploiter and exploited: beads are traded for gold. Later it becomes more two-directional: refrigerators for gold. Then popular imagery spreads, usually from the center of greater wealth: Coca-colonialism, Marlboro ads, Marilyn, Elvis. Finally high imagery flows: our high art and theirs mutually merge in a series of uneven steps. If one understands art as an expression of the identity of a culture, then the artwork might be seen as an embodiment of the culture's soul. When different arts flow into one another, it is as if the souls of cultures are merging. The merging of Sumerian and Egyptian icons in ancient Near Eastern cultures subject to influence from both, the merging of Greek sculptural forms into Indian Buddhism, the back-and-forth influence between postwar American and Japanese cultures—these are examples of that process.

A Question. This dialogue of objects is a channel for a type of communication that was missing in the

colonial period and the generation or two of its aftermath. In that era, even ethnographic writing, for all
its intentions of neutrality and objectivity, was generally uni-ocular: the gaze went all one way. *We* represented *them* in *our* ways of representation. What
resulted was often either Western discourse applied
blindly outside its sphere of relevance, or, in perhaps
the most sensitive cases, what Clifford Geertz has
called "haunted reflections on Otherness."[10] James
Clifford has written of the need for ethnographic
discourse to become a dialogue in which the identities
of both observer and observed are in question—that
is, in which each party is open to influence, to being
changed inwardly, by the other—as opposed to "discourses that portray the cultural realities of other peoples without placing their own reality in jeopardy."[11]
Will the long-insular world of Western contemporary
art receive contemporary art from previously colonized cultures with such openness? At least the development of such dialogue is finding, after long
drought, some advocates among white representa-
tives of Western institutions.

   It is a difficult task to find ways into this project,
with the cloud of colonial history still lying so dark
and heavy over attempts at communication. One ex-
ploration is Robert Farris Thompson's study of the
responses of African artists to reproductions of Cub-
ist paintings. Another is the exhibition *Africa Explores: 20th Century African Art,* which proposes a
dialogue not only of objects but of their makers.
These African works came to us in the West carrying
within them memories of works of ours that went

out to them some years ago, works that themselves carried memories of African works from a yet earlier passage. Insofar as art is an expression of cultural identity, this work is a critique of our identity through the conflation of elements of *us* with elements of *them*. Both of the art traditions involved in the dialogue will be abused in the process, torn out of their intended limits, out of their sense of themselves as they thought they knew themselves to be. Both will be used in misconceived or Other-conceived juxtapositions that mock their initial intentions. As art is the symbol of the self, the self will be symbolically torn and distorted in this exchange, made a monstrous pastiche again. Yet in the articulation of their difference, a sameness emerges, too, from their conflation in one new monstrous being.

Cognitive Baptism. In the 16th and 17th centuries, the conquest of non-Western peoples by European armies was justified by Christianity, which posited the mission of baptizing the heathen in order to save them from eternal damnation. (Like Aristotle's denial of the humanness of Scythians, this justification for foreign conquest is quite ancient; it goes back to Zoroastrian arguments in support of the Persian Empire in the 6th century BC.) This archaic reasoning lost plausibility with the secularization of Europe in the 18th century but was soon replaced by another, articulated most fully and systematically in Kant's *Critiques*. There one finds the doctrine of the three faculties, the cognitive, the ethical, and the esthetic, that are said to make up the human as a receptor and processor of information, and the all-important insistence that they have nothing to do with one another. None of them, according to Kant, can confirm or reject the judgments of another. Like senses, each has its proper sphere, in which its judgments are final and authoritative. As one cannot hear the color red, so one cannot cognitively determine whether an ethical or esthetic judgment has been properly made, and so on.

This doctrine served to elevate European culture over other cultures—and thus to assure that it had not only the right but the responsibility to conquer them—by arguing that European judgments and the process by which they were reached were superior to those of other cultures. Kant's description of the three faculties on the lines of the senses was designed to make the exercise of any one of them as direct and incontrovertible as a judgment of sense. Skeptical epistemologists have opined that the only indubitable statements are to the effect that, "I feel cold," or, "I seem to see the color red."[12] No argument or testimony can refute such statements as long as they are sincerely made. Kant, with his recognition of the inaccessibility of the thing in itself, nevertheless tried to fashion a theory of knowledge that would let our apprehensions get as close to it as possible, and fashioned this theory on the model of such sense-based statements. On the basis of Kant's epistemology, Western philosophers developed a feeling that their cognitions were the best that could be attained with human apparatus. This assurance spread through

Western society and tacitly supported the violent progress of 19th- and 20th-century imperialisms.

Kant's theory of knowledge, then, implicitly rejects the cognitive formations of non-Western cultures. The Western judgment on art, for example, was said to be exclusively esthetic, when properly exercised, with no clouding by social or cognitive concerns. In contrast, the members of traditional societies, in which art is said to exist in the matrix of religion and communal rite, were thought to experience the esthetic along with the social and the cognitive. In terms of Kantian theory, this was a confused way of receiving artistic experience. This view of the inadequacy of the perceptions and cognitions of non-Western peoples was akin to the Christian view of their soullessness and to Hegel's view that Oriental cultures are "for the most part really unhistorical"[13]—that is, outside of the story of the human. (Yet in Western post-Modernism of the last decade or two, the tripartite approach to art prevalent in pre-Modern cultures—with esthetic, social, and cognitive elements conflated and interpenetrated—has returned.)

Knowledges. One would think that a post-colonial attitude must acknowledge different theories of knowledge, including some that imply the falsity of one's own inherited assumptions. One is bound, in other words, to betray one's own specific ethnic inheritance in the attempt to open oneself to the reality of others—"to try to do away with my own presence," as Todorov says, "'for the other's sake'."[14] Thus, the Western decolonialist would enter the same realm of monstrosity inhabited by Sartre's complicit colonial.

Acknowledging a variety of conflicting theories as equal approaches to reality of course precludes any attempt to establish an objective or universal scale of certainty. Matters of truth and its security of self become accepted simply as parts of what Michel Foucault called the game of truth and falsity.[15] So in attempting to get into a post-colonialist (as distinct from neo-colonialist) frame of mind, both the European and the African must develop the ability to switch value frameworks and cognitive frameworks at will.

There are common cognitive acts which parallel this idea. Suppose, for example, that one is presented with a sheet of paper that has markings on it and is then questioned about its quality. One will first have to know what the markings are intended to be. If they are identified as a poem, let's say, they may seem very bad, but when they are identified as a cartoon they may be judged to be very good; if they are identified as a drawing in the high art sense they may seem mediocre, as a map, abominable, and so on. Similarly a post-Modern epistemology involves a constantly shifting identity such that one could say, If I were a Zulu I might say this work is not so good; If I were a French aristocrat, hey, it's great; an ancient Egyptian, run of the mill; an American entrepreneur, simply boring—and so on. Thus the etic attitude is not singular and elevated above others, but a compendium of many emicnesses. (And what is one really, in the midst of this unanchored or rudderless sailing on cognitive seas? This one does not know yet.)

Representations. A part of the epistemological imperialism that sustained economic imperialism was the assumption that Western modes of representation, whether visual or otherwise, were superior— that is, more objective or true to nature than those of non-Western cultures. This would seem to be a simple emic assumption. As the naturalness of the given world view seems obvious in the emic situation, so does the naturalness of the inherited representations, visual and verbal, which embody that view. But can there be convincing arguments, other than the emic infatuation with one's own inherited ways, for the objectivity of one mode of representation over another? One Western artist concerned with this issue, Leonardo da Vinci, is said to have used a mirror to ascertain the accuracy of a drawing. Situating the mirror in relation to a still life or figure so it presented him with the same view that he was attempting to draw or paint, he would check to see, for instance, if a line exited the rectangle of the picture at the same point at which its reflection exited the rectangle of the mirror. Greek sculptors sometimes measured the dimensions of an object and made their representation of it with the same measurements. Much more recently, Yves Klein exhibited body casts of his subjects. Such methods would appear to provide some basis for claiming objectivity of representation—but that does not amount to certainty in the subjective realm. If you say, "This portrait doesn't look like that person to me," then, as with the statement, "I feel cold," there is no argument or test which can refute you.

The Modernist assumption that our representations were true to nature and those of others were not, suggested that other peoples were not seeing nature clearly. This reinforced epistemological questions about the value of their cognitions. Clearly, it seemed, other peoples were trying to see nature objectively—that is, the way we did—and we would be doing them a big favor by helping them. To do this, however, we had to convince them that their own representations were false and shameful. We had to turn them against their own ethnicity—that is, to a degree, against themselves. In the project of relativization, however, it is not only the Other but ourselves who are subverted.

Selves. To enter a dialogue in which one's own world view is on the line—to jettison one's inherited role in the game of truth and falsity—is to give up one's patrimony in the world, which is to say one's selfhood. Insofar as the self is ethnically constituted the project of fetishizing difference in one's own person is like changing one's unconscious mind.

One of the common social functions of art has been its role in shaping and sustaining the sense of identity (hence, in changing it). Art presents communally generated and communally received objects that invite a bonding of communal identification around a shared understanding of their meaning. Its long association with totemic representation illustrates this function of sustaining a highly focused sense of identity. Yet as an instrument of persuasion, art has the ability to sever as well as to bond, and to rebond in new associations of cultural pastiche.

Sartre's idea of the monstrosity of the converted colonial assumes the existance of an integral self that should not be invaded and remade, should not be violated, by another self. But isn't it perhaps better, more realistic, to be unsure who you are? The Zairian idea of "authenticity" (like the "negritude" idea from Senegal, and other phenomena of post-colonial recovery of balance) expresses an insistence on the self and its endurance. The post-Modern emphasis on the de-centering of the self, in contrast, implies an affirmation of cultural pastiche, the self diffused through all cultures, as once the self of the Sorcerer of Trois Freres, portrayed on a Magdalenian cavern wall some 20,000 years ago, diffused itself through all nature, assuming at once the attributes of bird, bear, feline, and horned beast.

Invisible? "How do we explain the total ignorance about the achievement of non-European artists in the West? Why are they invisible?" asks Rasheed Araeen.[16] A theoretical answer based on Hegel might be, "Because they're nature, not culture." This part of the Modernist ideology of world mastery is similar to the Witotos' declaration that all other human groups are Peoples of the Animals, and it is one of the colonialist dichotomies that is changing most radically in the post-Modern turn. Fredric Jameson defines late capitalism— that is, the age when Modernism gives way to post-Modernism—as the period when "the last vestiges of Nature which survived on into classical capitalism are at last eliminated: namely the third world and the unconscious."[17] With ethnicity—a reality that lies somewhere between the personal and the universal—replacing both the personal unconscious and communal unconscious as the upsurging element of surprised self-recognition, the distinction between nature and culture is going fast too. (That distinction, which goes back to the Greek Sophists as a part of the cover story for an earlier colonial period, was based on the assumption that culture could be controlled but nature could not; now that situation seems directly reversed.)

In Hegelian terms, when members of non-Western cultures begin to adopt Western styles, they are ceasing to be nature and becoming culture. But by the same token, as they become, as it were, eticized and supposedly more like us, they do not become more controllable but less so. Their situation *and* ours are both changing out of control. And the search for the Other then is a search for the newness of one's changing self.

Talkin' 'Bout Us. "The cultures of world peoples need to be constantly rediscovered," wrote George Marcus and Michael Fischer, "as these peoples reinvent them in changing historical circumstances...."[18] This sentence may seem to refer primarily to *others,* but it holds for *us,* too, as we seek to know ourselves in the midst of an unexpected and unpredictable change. From the point of view of a Westerner with all the accumulated and interwoven karma of Christianity, imperialism, and Coca-Cola, the distinction between Modernism and post-Modernism seems deeply significant, indeed almost salvific, a feeling traditionally associated with rites of rebirth and other assertions of new selfhood. (That is the danger in the terms Modern and post-Modern—they may imply too much; but even the numbers of the years, being based on the Christian era, are value-saturated.) It is in part through our representations, their mergers and borrowings and adaptations, that our identities are shifted into new forms, and this is why the advent of post-Modernism in the West has been experienced prominently as a crisis in our representations.

In the Modernist period we in the West thought our representations were more real than the representations of other cultures. We were living in a dream which was peopled and propped by our representations. Now we wake up—or think we wake up but we may still be in just another dream, maybe a framing dream or maybe a detail, we can't tell yet. Anyway, seeming to awaken, we embarrassedly see that our inherited modes of representation were not more real than others' in a general sense; they only seemed more real to us. They were tribal, and like damn fools we thought they were universal. And it was so easy to do that. The belief that one's representations are etic is the most characteristic of all emic simplicities. Cut loose from the anchors of our ignorance, we float rudderless on a sea of the real-with-out-name. And we call it post-Modernism, a name which has the advantage of being a non-name, a concept shaped by negation rather than by position. (Modernism was all about position.)

But is there a non-position which is not also a position? Is there an etic stance which is not also emic? "They stand firmly because they stand no-where," says Subhuti in describing the Bodhisattvas. We too wish to stand firmly yet stand nowhere, to act as two rather than as one, to incorporate difference into the felt sameness of existence. Between presence and represence—to paraphrase T.S. Eliot—falls the shadow. Things blur into universals, experiences into metaphors, objects into objective correlatives. In a sense, to stand in two places is to stand both in presence and in representation. For representations are not simply less real than what they represent; they are also real in that, as Paul Rabinow observed, "representations are social facts."[19] They are not, in other words, just *re*presences, but presences. They are parts of ourselves. The crisis of representation, then, is a potential opening into new modes of selfhood. The danger is that the crisis of representation might be just another representation—just another device for modelling reality into manageable scale.

NOTES

1. For an unpacking of this sentence, see Thomas McEvilley, "Art History or Sacred History?," *Art & Discontent,* Kingston, NY: Documentext/McPherson & Company, 1991.

2. Kumkum Sangari, "Representations in History," *Journal of Arts and Ideas* nos. 17 & 18, New Delhi: June, 1989, p. 4.

3. For a critique of the view of African art as timeless or ahistorical see Susan Vogel, "Digesting the West," in Susan Vogel, *Africa Explores: 20th Century African Art,* New York: The Center for African Art, 1991, pp. 14–31.

4. See William Rubin, ed., *"Primitivism" in 20th Century Art: Affinity of the Tribal and the Modern,* New York: The Museum of Modern Art, 1984.

5. The Expression Theory of art implies that the object, since it is said to express something, is actually a kind of subject, an animate being possessing preferences about what it is assumed to be expressing. If an artifact or art object were truly inanimate, it would seem that the projection of one thought value or another upon it would be as much a matter of indifference to the object as the way one regards a stone is to a stone.

6. I am indebted to the anthropologist Juan Echeverri for this and other information about the Witoto.

7. My use of the terms emic and etic is based on the discussion by Marvin Harris in *Cultural Materialism,* New York: Random House [Vintage], 1980, p. 32ff.

8. Badri Raina, "The Politics of Development," *Journal of Arts and Ideas* nos. 17 & 18, New Delhi: June, 1989, p. 96.

9. Sangari, " Representations in History," p. 4.

10. Clifford Geertz, *Works and Lives: The Anthropologist as Author,* Stanford, CA: Stanford University Press, 1988, p. 16.

11. James Clifford, "On Ethnographic Authority," *Representations* I no. 2, 1983, p. 133.

12. A.J. Ayer, *The Problem of Knowledge,* New York: Penguin, 1977, pp. 54–56.

13. *The Philosophy of History,* New York: Dover, 1956, p. 106.

14. Cited by Michael M.J. Fischer in "Ethnicity and the Post-Modern Arts of Memory," in Clifford and Marcus, eds., *Writing Culture,* Berkeley, CA: Univ. of California Press, 1986, p. 201: quotes Tzve-

tan Todorov, *The Conquest of America: The Question of the Other*, New York: Harper & Row, 1984 [1982], pp. 250–251.

15. Michel Foucault, "Truth and Power," in C. Gordon, ed., *Power/ Knowledge: Selected Interviews and Other Writings, 1972–1977*, New York: Pantheon, 1980.

16. Rasheed Araeen, "Our Bauhaus Others' Mudhouse," *Third Text: Third World Perspectives on Contemporary Art and Culture* no. 6, Spring, 1989, pp. 12–13.

17. Cited by Paul Rabinow, "Representations Are Social Facts," p. 247: quotes Fredric Jameson, "Postmodernism and Consumer Society" in H. Foster, ed., *The Anti-Aesthetic: Essays on Postmodern Culture*, Port Townsend, WA: Bay Press, 1983, p. 207.

18. George E. Marcus and Michael M.J. Fischer, *Anthropology as Cultural Critique: An Experimental Moment in the Human Sciences*, Chicago: The University of Chicago Press, 1986, p. 24.

19. See note 17 above.

The Common Air

Contemporary Art in India

Our English host was gracious
We were soon at ease;
Or almost:
The servants
Were watching.
—Gieve Patel, Evening

It took me a long time to see that de Kooning was not
merely undisciplined.—Bikash Bhattacharjee

India is like an immense dark space in our imagination: we feel it lying hidden in a part of our minds where we store things too big and "other" to absorb—in the unconscious, or in that shadowy area of consciousness in which we relate to concepts like infinity, outer space, the sublime, or the underworld. For thousands of years, Westerners seeking something unknown and unnameable have been drawn there. Long before Mia Farrow and the Beatles, the Greeks and Romans climbed the hills to gurus' caves. In the '60s, many went there, often artists and writers; by the '80s, many more were making the trip. Throughout our century, really, from E.M. Forster to Francesco Clemente, this visit to the unconscious of our own imagination has established a sense of the outer limits of Western culture, showing us what we are not, offering us a freedom from our own traps of history and identity. What people bring back is shock and thrill and changed lives. They've seen and felt something that lies outside our grids of order and patterns of values, something that seems timeless, like the ocean, and that has the power to rearrange the Western mind.

India's all-absorbing contradictions are not accessible anywhere else, except, perhaps, deep in ourselves. Its neolithic villages spill naked tribal people into overcrowded urban streets where yogis brush by businessmen in Western suits, while lepers creep to taxicab windows to beg. The country's overwhelming combination of beauty and horror opens into dizzying reaches of anonymity: the masses. The British, at once fascinated and repelled by India's uncontrollable vastness, feared the seductive loss of self that was offered by the experience of "going native," of losing one's grip on Western civilization and history, and descending into an adventure without end or purpose. More recently, it seems, many of us who visit India go precisely in order to loose that tired grip, or to break its oppressive force. Meanwhile, India, while offering us a way out of history, suffers and acts within its own history, a history that seems to feature fatality and cyclicity, that is always surging like the waves. Caught in the endless rounds of its cycles, India gazes at moments toward the West, hungering to participate in the Western feeling of history, with its appearance of purpose and linear direction. India and the West, the West and India— we are what each other's imaginations are seeking.

India has endured several thousand years of repeated foreign conquest and frequent foreign rule. Its culture—despite the intensity of its selfhood, its gravity as itself—has functioned as a receptive membrane upon which other cultures have left their foreign imprints. The result is a society characterized by uneven development and layered with a pluralism beyond Western imagination. The coin room of the Indian Museum, Calcutta, tells the story. In chronological sequence, it holds Persian coins, Greek coins, Kushan coins, Sassanid coins, Hina coins, then, for a rare change, the coins of the native Indian dynasty called Gupta, followed by Muslim coins, and, for a long two centuries, the coins of the British. The prehistoric Dravidian migrations were followed, at the dawn of Indian history, by the Aryan invasions, which were followed in turn by Persian conquerors, then by the conquest of much of India by Greek monarchs, the Greeks being succeeded by a variety of Central Asian invaders and rulers. Muslim invasions in the Middle Ages led to centuries of rule by often warring foreign dynasties, until the British, after episodes of Portuguese, Dutch, and French commercial exploitation, got rid of the Muslim rulers in their turn. Each of these elements took from India and became a part of it.

In art, the heritage of Hindu temple sculpture, say, lies alongside Central Asian art of various kinds, Mogul miniatures, 19th-century British realism, and currents of 20th-century European and American influences as well as earlier European ones, particularly that of the Renaissance. India was a post-Modern culture before it was a Modern one. The spatial vastness of the country contains as much variety, contradiction, and conflict as does its layered heritage. In addition to the basic division between the north, roughly Aryan, and the south, roughly Dravidian, regions such as the Punjab, Bengal, and Gujarat are semiautonomous cultural zones, each with its own languages, its own stories, its own music, its own style of dance, and so on. For hundreds of years the Indian mind has had access to a complex amalgam of cultural paradigms without needing to go beyond India itself. Long before Nietzsche declared that the Modern Age in the West would be an age of comparison, something like that situation existed in India.

An array of inherited cultural elements—literary, philosophical, religious, artistic, and so on—together make up what in India is called the Tradition. In the visual arts today this complexity is mirrored forth with startling clarity. One may practice the Tradition by practicing any part of it in the prescribed way. Though Hindu elements are at the very center of the Tradition, all its features are ultimately seen as Indian. One may paint miniatures in the Mogul style or portraiture in the 19th-century British style and in either case one's work is Indian. The history of Indian art in the last century has been a history of changing modes of relating to the Tradition.

The various traditions that coexist within the Tradition in the larger sense have until recently resisted assimilation with each other, maintaining themselves in isolated sectarian schools, each puristically practicing its particular mode. In many of the colleges of art, for example, these divisions are still rigorously maintained. A "painting" course means 19th-century-style British academic realism, mostly portraiture. Students standing before turn-of-the-century-style easels produce paintings practically identical, as if from one hand, and often dark like Old Master paintings; the darkness legitimizes them, making them look like the reproductions of old European paintings that hang around the hallways and staircase landings of the colleges. A course in "Indian-style painting" is very different: students sitting on mats on the floor make copies and imitations of Mogul miniatures. Both groups are apt to be proficient, but always within a strictly delimited inherited style. Most often, there has been no mingling of styles. Similarly, in a school of sculpture near Madras ("the best in India," said my guide, "and maybe the world"), dozens of young stone-cutters make more or less exact copies of traditional Hindu temple sculptures, maintaining the style with no sign that any cross-currents exist in their world.

A break in this situation in fine art began to appear with the Bengali cultural movement early in this century. In an influential essay of 1921, still reprinted, on "The Meaning of Art," Rabindranath Tagore, the great Bengali poet, educator, and theorist of art, referred to the various art traditions that had established themselves in India as "masks with exaggerated grimaces, that fail to respond to the ever changing play of life." Indian artists, he wrote, should set themselves free from their multitude of inherited styles, each sheltered in its own academy. They were to stop limiting their production to the various established branches of the Tradition. At the time he wrote this, aged around 60, Tagore had begun to produce paintings that "approximated the work of some of the *avant-garde* modern artists of the West," in the words of one Indian commentator. The National Gallery of Modern Art, Delhi, has room after room of these. But the Western Modernist influence on Tagore's work is not the whole story. He did not neglect his Indianness, but, in a mood profoundly prophetic for later Indian art, spoke in the same essay of being "naturally Indian in spite of all the borrowings that [we] indulged in." In India, the paintings of Tagore are esteemed like sacred icons, and with reason. For all his loving attention to the Indian tradition, Tagore threw the lightning bolt by saying that art must at the same time be national and transcend nationalism, be local and worldwide.

The impulse toward internationalism that appeared in a mild form in the Bengali movement gained momentum when India became self-ruling, for the first time in about a thousand years, in 1947, adopting a democratic constitution for the first time in its long history. Around this time, self-conscious assertions of Indian cultural Modernism began to be made. The most famous occurred in the same historic year. A group of artists in Bombay issued a manifesto, calling themselves the Bombay Progressive Artists Group. They were immediately acknowledged by artists who shared their attitude, in Calcutta and elsewhere. The Bombay Progressives unabashedly recommended the adoption of the styles and modes of European Modern art, specifically the School of Paris. Certain of them also advocated abstraction, with an ideology essentially formalist in the Western mode, decrying subject matter and insisting that only attention paid to line and color was valid. India had produced abstract art before—notably in the various 18th-century Tantric schools—but for two thousand years Indian art had been primarily an art of the figure. With the Bombay Progressives, it took a turn regarded by many of these artists' compatriots as a rejection of the Tradition, even though much of their work continued to employ vestigial references to Hindu signs of a variety of kinds.

Despite the unquestioned impact of the Bombay Progressives on Indian culture, Modernist abstract painting did not catch on widely there. A number of early abstractionists have since become figurative painters, as have most of the artists of the generation that followed; among prominent Indian artists today, Sayed Haider Raza, V.S. Gaitonde, and Ram Kumar (born 1923, 1924, and 1924 respectively) are among the few who remain abstractionists. The revolutionary and problematic relationship to the Indian identity adopted by the Progressives was exacerbated by the fact that many of them left India soon after the formation of the group, some staying in the West for long periods of time or permanently. As

Tagore had thrown the lightning bolt, this generation felt its heat and were propelled by its impact
much farther into internationalism than Tagore himself was ready to go. The abstract work of the Progressives ranges from Raza's mild tachism with hints
of Tantra, to the vaguely mottled surfaces, redolent
of spirituality, of Gaitonde's canvases, to Kumar's
competent late-Abstract-Expressionism-like paintings. Raza has lived in Paris since 1949; Kumar spent
a long time in that city, where he studied under Fer-
nand Léger and knew Paul Eluard, but now lives in
India again, and Gaitonde has remained in India.
Figurative work by the Progressives tends to feature
indigenous scenes painted in styles that verge on the
abstract. It ranges from the early village-art-like illustration of M. F. Husain (born 1915), and his sophisticated later imitations of movie billboards and
photographs of Indian street scenes, to F. N. Souza's
scenes from Hindu mythology, in treatments remi-
niscent of Paul Klee and Marc Chagall. Souza (born
1924) was the actual founder of the Bombay Progressives, and wrote its manifestos.

It's difficult to exaggerate the importance of the
generation of the Bombay Progressives, with their
post-Tagorean denunciation of exclusive Indianness
for its own sake, their affirmation of internationalism, and their attempt to come to terms with the
School of Paris. In the '40s in India, the idea of doing
something that did not grow out of and above all
receive legitimation from some part of the inherited
Tradition seemed an outrageous or atrocious idea.
Then a handful of people, with no following, no

sanction from any authority or institution, and no justification in terms of their own culture adopted Modern art. It was an attempt to close the gap between India and the West in one breath-taking step. A certain wishful element seems involved, and the mechanism of the wish was based on the Modernist concept of universality. It seemed for a brief time that one could enter history on the same footing as everyone else if one tuned one's sensibility to the Modern universals. This step away from the cumbersome weight of inherited, externally imposed traditions held momentous promise. Tyeb Mehta (born 1925), a painter of the generation of the Bombay Progressives whose work is of great importance today, once said, "It took courage, at that time, to pick up a brush, to make a mark on a canvas"—a mark, in other words, that was not this or that inherited icon or word or symbol, a mark expressing a sense of what it feels like to be outside a tradition or a rule, to be an individual expressing one's own sensibility. At the moment that someone lifted that brush and made that mark, a part of Indian culture entered the modern world—for better or for worse.

Still, Western viewers may have problems in accepting this and other Indian work that derives its look in part from Western models. When seeing Mehta's thrilling oil paintings, for example, which to Western eyes recall the late paper-cutout works of Henri Matisse, or the beautiful paintings on glass by K. G. Subramanyan, which recall earlier works by Matisse, we find ourselves asking what the value is of having more Matisse-like work long after Matisse. But the question of chronology—who was first in making things that look like that? —needs to be viewed within the larger context of cultural diffusion. Early in this century European artists adopted the styles of alien, primarily Oceanic and African cultures, not as momentary quotations but as lasting permeations of their styles, which supposedly arose from their selves. The fact that a style of African mask may have been made for centuries in Africa did not lead us to denounce Pablo Picasso as derivative for imitating it at a time when it was old, even classical, in its own context. To an extent, this was because the African look was a new experience for us, as the Matissean one may be for Indians. As the borrowing culture, we felt enriched; now, as the lending culture, we seem to feel superior. But it must be stressed that the history of diffusion rarely follows chronological niceties; as a transfer of elements from one culture to another, diffusion necessarily confuses. This is how a civilization spreads and grows. Ultimately, the whole issue of the newness of art is involved, for in a sense, of course, all art is derived from sources, and most culture is made up in large part of elements once diffused in chaotic recombinations from elsewhere. Finally, it should be said that in asking who made something that looked a certain way first, we are asking a question that in a global world, where all elements are laid out on the table, is surely dead. We can see the African model that moved Picasso, and we can see the Matissean model that moved someone else. The useful question now is not who first thought of the look, but what did each culture or artist do with the look, how it was used, contextualized, filled with meaning—how it functioned.

In India, some artists of the generation of the Progressives shied away from the danger of appearing to submit so directly to foreign influences. Amrita Sher-Gil (1913–1941) and others developed types of figuration rooted in Indian village life. K.C.S. Paniker (1911–1977) developed, in the '60s, a form of abstraction that has come to be called Neo-Tantric. Neo-Tantra makes a gesture of sympathy toward Modernism while remaining far more tightly bound to the Tradition than does the relatively free abstraction of some of the Progressives. Paniker chose not to follow Western models of abstraction directly but to base his work on abstract art already existing in the Tradition, the cosmograms and meditative abstractions known loosely as yantras.

Other Neo-Tantric artists, while motivated by Paniker's example, shifted emphasis in various ways. Om Prakash (born 1932) makes luscious axial-symmetrical abstractions, with names like *Glorified Seed,* 1984. The paintings of K.V. Haridasan (born 1937) have a sophisticated relationship to American Hard Edge abstraction along with their Yogic intentions and yantric derivation. The '60s work of J. Swaminathan (born 1929) is related to that of Paniker but wilder, inspired by a desire to blow apart the emerging consensus on School-of-Paris taste that the Bombay Progressives had put in place. Neo-Tantra is also somewhat contradictory insofar as some of its practitioners associate it with the idea of an age when art was a cultic, socially integrated function—the Western analogy would be the age of the cathedrals—yet the work functions quite differently in its own setting, where some of the artists, for example, sign their works, exhibit them in galleries, and sell them for individual gain. Still, within the Indian framework—and things have their own meaning within their own frameworks—this art, in the '60s and early '70s, the age of Color Field, Hard Edge, and Minimal painting in the West, was a feasible solution to the problem of maintaining Indianness while not totally rejecting Modern influence.

Traditionally, Hinduism has regarded itself as transcending history. Modernism and Modern art represent history. Behind the distinction between the Progressives and the Neo-Tantrists lie different senses of identity, the one willing to submerge the Indian identity in an international identity based on alleged artistic universals, the other based on Indian traditions and on an insistence that they have meaning and power apart from participation in the world community. Both of these movements go on.

The generation of artists born mostly around 1940 ignored the barriers between the various purisms and chose from each whatever they wanted, combining elements without regard to origin. They freely mingled ideas from Western art, from the Renaissance to Modernism, with the Persian, Mogul, and other influences that are part of the fabric of India itself. Out of this stew a new, more complex, and critical voice for Indian art—primarily Indian painting—is emerging.

The recent work of Gulam Mohammed Sheikh (born 1937) centers around the theme of "returning home"—that is, of finding an Indian identity again. His paintings are actively and complexly quotational. In *About Waiting and Wandering*, 1981, a Piero della Francesca madonna appears in company with an architectural scene based on Ambrogio Lorenzetti's *Allegory of Good Government*, ca. 1338–48. In *Revolving Routes*, 1981, we see August Rodin's *Thinker*, a floating figure from Chagall. In *Untitled*, 1985, an angel from a Persian miniature flies by.

Sheikh's work illustrates some of the ways in which an experience of contemporary Indian art may be illuminating to us in the West. Its startling combinations of elements from Eastern and Western classicisms is based on a perception, derived from art history, of the relativity of realisms. Both European and Chinese art, Sheikh remarks, have arrived at styles that have a claim to being called realistic—yet these styles are very different. Just as the diffusion patterns that bring diverse cultural elements into India may indicate to us the relativity of our own developmental sequences, similarly this confrontation with a variety of realisms may show us the relativity of our own acculturated sense of what's real. A generation ago the Mogul method of representing architecture without the convergence of parallels toward a vanishing point appeared primitive in a Western culture habituated to the conventions of Renaissance perspective. Today, our own sense of spatial reality has pulled somewhat toward the Mogul, as architectural drawing has come to emphasize the axonometric rendering, in which parallels do not converge and the more distant parts of a building are as large on the page as the nearest.

Vivan Sundaram (born 1943) and many others of his generation wish to see the figure within its social environment, which is the radically uneven and changing face of India. His work continually contrasts the old and the new India, but without assuming that the new India has yet clearly revealed itself. In *Portrait of Father,* 1980, the male figure, off-center in its Western business suit, seems both isolated and forbidding. There is a mystery to what lies behind his eyes: are his thought patterns Westernized? Where has he hidden the Indian in himself? *Thinking about Themselves,* 1981, shows three women in an intimate setting, not conversing but almost as if posing for a camera. In the dreamy enclosedness of the women's quarters, and in the complexity of their dress—one in a sari, one in Punjabi garb, one possibly in Western clothing—are suggestions of the isolation of India, of its enclosure in the private dream of the Tradition, and of the variety of conflicting forces pulling it in different directions.

Though there is a similarity between the practice of these Indian artists and Western quotational art, the differences are perhaps even greater. Quotational art in Europe and America contains elements of homage, but usually the dominant tone has been one of criticism of art-historical notions of originality, of style, of the nature of movements in art, and especially of progress, an idea that in the Modernist emphasis became formulaic. By holding up for neutral inspection the esthetic or representational canons of the past, out of context and stripped of their aura, the artist is often asking us to perceive the limits of those canons. In the work of Sheikh and Sundaram quotation is less critical and ironic; it functions more as a way of putting oneself in a context, of making the roots of one's art an open part of it.

A still younger generation is focusing even more freely on issues of cultural identity without the sense of exclusive adherence to either abstraction or representation. Chandrasen M. Salvi (born 1960), for example, exhibited a complex multi-panelled work in 1985 that hovered bewilderingly among the genres of abstract art, representational art, Pop art, graphic design, and Conceptual art. The question of Indian identity—the "Indianness" of the work—was approached through a series of transformations of the Indian flag, inspired, says the artist, by Jasper Johns's treatment of the American one.

These and other artists have compacted into the recent and current art history of India a kind of paradigm, compressed into a few years, of the issues of art and cultural identity in general. When a culture that has been deeply engrossed in its own tradition has contacts with the different customs of a variety of foreign cultures, either it builds a wall, usually only mental, around itself to fend off foreign influences, which are seen as innately threatening (because they are "other"), or it attains an understanding of the reality of its own customs and, with that, the beginning of a gradual expansion through the incorporation of foreign elements into itself. The diffusion of artistic styles and motifs is one of the most visible and volatile elements in the latter choice, because it seems to break down the identities of traditional cultures. The Progressives made the necessary radical beginning, sacrificing their personal identification with the Tradition because not to do so meant clinging to, and reinforcing, what V.S. Naipaul called a "wounded civilization." To them, Modernism was a call. Some experienced it as a mighty force that drew them away from home, in a process as radical and unforgiving as a storm. Not much of self—understood as the sedimentation of one's past—was left to the Progressives. Then the next generation, having been effectually set free by the Progressives, found that it was no longer necessary to leave home, and began weaving out of old materials a new story for India, seeking among the broken pieces its new face, its new artistic spirit. They attempted to return their art home. But having been abroad, it brought new gifts, new baggage. One never returns home as one left it, and hence home can never be experienced again exactly as we remember leaving it. It is perhaps in the midst of catastrophic change, or in a time of anguished endings and beginnings, that artists have the greatest opportunity to offer something of crucial value to the culture around them, by seeking, through the image, ways to deal with the destruction of an old identity and to begin to shadow forth a new one.

In Europe and America, we too have been groping recently for new ways to relate to our tradition, and have been infusing it with loan elements from other cultures to open it up in directions now closed to it. As with Indian artists, Western artists have turned to a variety of sources of new elements, among them Japan and India. Many Western artists have gone to India in the last thirty years, some of them many times. Most of them do not relate directly to contemporary Indian art while they are there, but take home elements from India's past, as Indian artists have from our past. Some Western artists collaborate with Indian craftspeople. Some bring new ranges of color into their work, new strangenesses of images, new feelings of light and dark, new feelings for materials—including fabrics, papers, and metals—and new stylistic influences or borrowings, like Clemente's Mogul-like miniatures and his references to Hindu mythology, or Howard Hodgkin's incorporation of Rajput and Mogul influences. There is, in addition, a body of work by Westerners that is merely derivative kitsch or psychedelia or empty Tantricism.

These passages between Eastern and Western cultures are parts of a vast array of intercultural transactions in the world today which together comprise a great process of reorganization and seeking. In a shrinking yet terrifying world, we have to learn— and use—each other's languages, for the future is an unknown language that we will compose together.

One Culture of Many Cultures

The formalist or esthetic era of art bore within it a little-regarded contradiction: it featured the idea of change, but put no value on change for its own sake, imagining it instead as a movement toward some kind of end or culmination of history. What wasn't realized was that, if no such conclusion were forthcoming, these endless changes would become mutually trivializing. If a great artistic innovation is going to last only a few years or months, what really is the value of it? Shall history be rewritten for such a transient consummation? Are historical periods to become mere fads? In this way the formalists, who intended to affirm the high seriousness of art, ended by diminishing it. The proliferation of terminology to designate supposedly new styles and schools was kept going by a residual formalist habit even after formalism had supposedly ended. It soon became a joke: action painting, Color Field, Hard Edge, Pop art, Op art, Minimal art, Conceptual art, earth art, body art, Happenings, performance art, primary shapes, photorealism, new image, bad

127

painting, pluralism, Neo-Expressionism, simulation-
ism, Neo-Geo, neo-Conceptualism.

Even in the '80s, when formalism was busily dis-
sected everywhere, this trivializing impetus continued to gain momentum as an overheated market
looked for a new ism every second year or so. By
about 1985, the idea that there might be more endur-
ing developments in the history of art had been ob-
scured. As the prefix "neo" suggests, history seemed
to have been reduced to absurdity. This loss of faith
in the advance of formalist moments reflected a
deeper loss of faith in the similarly discredited march
of technological moments, which had been the main
underpinning of Modernist faith in progress. In this
sense, art as previously known has not survived
Modernism. Post-Modernism seems to many to
have robbed art of its will by relativizing its values,
but it seems to me that the problem, if it is one, lies
in the lingering traces of formalist ways of thought.

After long periods of unquestioning belief, there
is a certain satisfaction in cynicism. It is somehow
liberating to see all things as equally trivial (as in
certain areas of Greek philosophy—Pyrrhonism, for
example—or in Madhyamika Buddhism). Thus, the
recent coinage "multi-culti," a mocking term for the
general intercultural tendencies in the arts today, can
draw a smile from most of us when inflected with
the proper wickedness. But the joke is far from trivial, for it reflects a general loss of faith in the importance of art and a suspicion that what happens in art
history has no real importance for anything except
the market. Specifically, it casts the group of tenden-

cies linked under the names post-Modernism, globalism, and multiculturalism (all more or less syno-
nyms in this context) as just another passing fad, no
more important than Neo-Geo, say, and no different
in scale. Beneath its humor, this tactic serves to disguise a conservative defense, which can be associated
with the remnants of formalism, against the threat
to the idea of quality that multiculturalism involves,
as well as against its threat to the idea of art history
as a thin linear stream of linked formal sequences.
But this defense is desperate and unreal. In fact,
something of a different scale entirely is happening
in multiculturalism, something that transcends the
succession of formalist moments and radically shifts
their emphasis.

The visual arts have a global social importance today that is quite independent of formalist notions of
esthetic presence. A culture's visual tradition embodies the image it has of itself. Cumulatively, and with
cross-currents, art draws into visibility from the
depths of intuition a culture's sense of its identity and
of its value and place in the world. Seen this way,
art—or visual expression or whatever we want to
call it—encompasses far more than esthetics. There
are times when the issue of identity is muted and the
esthetic voice speaks loudest. But not today. Right
now the issue of identity has come to the foreground
both of culture in general and of the visual in particular. This is not a stylistic fad; it involves the deepest
meanings of what we call history.

Viewed from the inside, European history since
the Renaissance has been a story of a step-by-step

articulation of a set of shifting yet coherent cultural forms—the working out of the identity of Europe through various sensual and intellectual modes. But viewed from outside, in a global framework, the same history suggests a very different story, one with two stages. The first is colonialism, which began in the Renaissance (the European enslavement of Africans started in the 15th century) and ended when the colonizing nations began to withdraw from their colonies, mostly in the middle decades of this century. The second stage, which is under way but still young, is the process of decolonialization, meaning not only the literal withdrawal of foreign armies and governments but the long aftermath of cultural readjustment. Decolonialization is undoubtedly the most significant global event at work today, with countries in both the Third World and Eastern Europe struggling to reclaim and reconstruct their ravaged cultural identities.

Multicultural projects in the visual arts are one branch of this historic process. A culture's visual tradition, when exported, is a kind of ambassador, and visual borrowings and mergings constitute a kind of foreign policy. The intermingling of different cultures' image banks as part of the post-colonial project is thus a sign of a deeper interpenetration of their identities. This was the inner meaning of the appropriation and quotation and so on of the '80s, which prepared the way for the multicultural '90s. The catchphrase "PC," like "multi-culti," is used to trivialize this development; but the true and serious meaning of the acronym is not so much "politically correct" as "post-colonial." In the move away from Modernism (colonialism), of course, post-Modernism (post-colonialism) does not begin with a clean slate. The idea of a historical change that leaves causality behind is a contradiction, since an acausal moment would of necessity be ahistorical. Still, history does strongly suggest the reality of what Gaston Bachelard and others have called *coupures épistemologiques*—epistemological breaks or gaps, moments in which things seem to change with a blinding flash, when the pebbles slowly shifting in the stream suddenly slide into a different shape, clog up the old passage, create new channels past a bottleneck, and spring forward with a momentary sense of freedom.

Part of the global project of decolonialization is a conscious effort—particularly on the part of white Westerners—to understand the image banks of other cultures. This will be no easy matter, since in many societies the inherited views about art and genius and so on have become parts of selfhood as it is felt. Inevitably, this adjustment involves ethnic considerations. In the Modernist period, when whites saw history as exclusively their own, African, Indian, Chinese, and Amerindian societies were regarded by white Westerners as ahistorical because they weren't dominated by the need to feel that they were evolving toward some ultimate consummation. Colonialism was justified as a means to drag the supposedly ahistorical into history—at which point non-European peoples were supposed to gradually become like Europeans or, more recently, European Americans. The otherness of the non-white would supposedly go away by being assimilated, as when Native Americans sported bowler hats and monocles in 18th-century American paintings.

But this whitening of the world was not to be. Instead, the white Westerner has been revealed as just another Other, with no special claim to being the self against which all are delineated or the standard to which it is the destiny of all to assimilate. Increasingly, it has become clear that in the emerging global scenario no one cultural form will be enforced on all. Instead, it will be one culture made of many cultures, one history made of many histories—a whole made of disunited fragments, with no imperative to unite them. Peoples clinging to their own heritages, traditions, languages, and styles of selfhood insist that they be written into history as themselves, and that their picture of us, with elements we might not relish, be written into that history too. Even more, they demand that they will write the history. Their cultural need, as Eboussi Boulaga put it, is "of being by and for oneself, through the articulation of having and making."*

* F. Eboussi Boulaga, *La Crise de Muntu,* Paris: Presence Africaine, 1977, p. 7.

A Time to Choose

Has the idea of "History" imploded, or has it simply taken new forms, like a natural species mutating for survival? In the realm of art, this question is currently reflected in matters of style.

The spate of abstract painting seen in New York in 1991 was largely created by young artists who do not directly remember either the single-minded intensity of Abstract Expressionism or, when it came, the emphatic consensus of agreement that the movement was over. Somehow, the style still seems to them a viable option (though only one of many), with or without the heavy baggage of the sublime.[1] One wonders, however, if this is not a somewhat unconsidered development. Even today, artists wishing to work in the fashion of one or two generations ago are usually expected to ground their practice in one historical stance or another. An artist still working out of an essentially Modernist approach, for example, might claim to address unfinished formal investigations that had perhaps been terminated prematurely—what George Kubler, in *The Shape of Time,* called open sequences. A post-Modernist, in contrast, might invoke a practice such as "quotation" or "simulation," in both of which an earlier style becomes a somewhat ironic signifier of a previous period, a locus for reflection rather than continued investigation. But the new abstraction seems to appear without such matrices of defense. One critic has told me he finds this art "irresponsible," implying that since art is inalienably embedded in history, to abandon historicity is not only a sign of sloppy thinking but a cop-out on the fullness of the art endeavor. Another, however, has celebrated this sense of irresponsibility with the declaration, "History is dead and everything is permitted."[2]

That author probably wrote with a certain irony. Still, he does describe the position that many of these young neo-abstractionists seem to assume: that they have no sense of history and no responsibility to it; that they are no longer required to set up their work in terms of a clear relationship to what has gone before and what might come after.

This position of free-fall is not, however, what I have been proposing to students lately in various art schools around the country. On the contrary, I have been telling them that now more than ever it is one of the artist's responsibilities to place his or her work clearly and deliberately *in* history—to reflect, that is, on what model of history the work presupposes, and on how it relates to that model. For it seems to me that what has happened in the post-Modern change of attitude might better be described not as the end of history and the resulting indefinite multiplication of options in an ahistorical free-for-all, but as the partial or temporary end of one view of history, and the consequent need to replace it with one or another of a variety of revisionist models.

Modernism was an ideological totality. It was an age when a single model of history seemed adequate to our experience—meaning the experience of white Westerners—and this model was basically the linear, progress-driven construct so influentially articulated by Hegel (though it existed long before him). History, in this view, can be visualized as a single line moving forward across the page of time, with the vast ahistorical blank spaces of nature and the undeveloped world all around it. Recently, this view has been discredited, in part by the fact that it accompanied and justified colonialism and imperialism. Those vast undeveloped spaces can no longer be relegated to an ahistorical limbo, nor will their inhabitants any longer accept a view of history that they understandably feel has victimized them.

Just as important, the idea that history's linear path reflects an inner purpose has become untenable. For the flow of events over this century seems to mock the very idea of a positive goal or end by its ever-increasing series of disasters. History's goal or end has come to seem a negative one; it has seemed to be taking us someplace we do not want to go, and—perhaps in the nick of time, perhaps too late—we have jumped ship.

But no new model has definitively established itself yet. We are in a suspended moment, with various possibilities available. That is why, now more than ever, it is essential that an artist, in order for his or her work to be meaningful, should aim it at one or another of these options. Otherwise, it occurs in an undefined space in which it might as well be a stick or a stone, needing no historical grounding or context because it makes no pretension to signification.

When the Modernist period seemed to come to an end, artists adopted a variety of adjustments. Some bailed out of Modernism into a kind of pre-Modern revival—"neo-pre-Modernism," perhaps—reflecting the flower-child ideology that was part of the social turmoil of the era's demise. In recent decades we have seen a broad-based desire to restore the spirituality of pre-Modern societies, with renewed emphases on ritual, ecology, and the feminine. In the art of the '60s and after, this impulse can be seen in ritual-based performance work (ranging from that of Hermann Nitsch to that of Donna Henes), earthworks with references to ancient monuments (such as those of Robert Smithson and Michael Heizer), shamanic re-readings of the role of the artist (as in the examples of Joseph Beuys and Ana Mendieta), and so on.

The models of history invoked by such works, however tacitly, are generally of two types. One is the idea of eternal cyclicity—the view of how events unfold characteristic of many pre-Modern societies. In the cyclic model of history, which involves rather less urgency and anxiety than the linear one, events come round again and again forever, like the rocking of a cosmic cradle. There can be no sense that one has missed the boat and will never have another chance. This cyclic view in turn takes two forms:

either events recur in exactly similar cycles, going round and round eternally like a closed circle on the page; or, more commonly, they have some element of linearity or directionality, moving across the page more like a coil or spiral than a circle. In the latter case, the question arises of the overall shape of the process. If the spiral is imagined to have a linear direction, then elements of Modernism are combined with the pre-Modern cyclicity; if, on the other hand, the spiral is viewed as basically circular or as part of a vaster spiral, other associations may be invoked, such as the sense of ever-expanding interpenetrating infinities in Avatamsaka Buddhism and elsewhere.

The second model of history invoked by some neo-pre-Modern work (such as some California light-and-space art and some Eastern-influenced performance) is the idea of an eternal present, which is harder to visualize as an image on a page but might equate with a single unmoving point, or perhaps with the blank page itself. This model is really ahistorical, and represents a retreat from the idea of history with a shape into the idea of featureless time.

Though the neo-pre-Modern option was most characteristic of the late '60s and early '70s, it is still with us, mostly in outlying areas where artists feel closer to nature than to culture. But other artists have chosen to treat the Modernist karma as still in force, for example, the early-'80s neo-expressionists or, in his recent work, Brice Marden. These artists still posit their works as proposals for sequential advancement through history via a continuing process of linked formal problems and solutions. Yet I think that even the most ardent of them lack the clear Modernist faith in the goal of it all; they carry the process forward in an almost self-sacrificial way, to keep open the channel to Heaven, as it were, despite troubling disturbances in the messages that flow through it. This residual Modernist model might be visualized as a straight line that continues past the so-called end of Modernism, but fades as it goes, becoming a kind of ghost of itself.

Perhaps more interesting than these approaches is an emerging set of post-Modernist models of history. Some artists, for example, have sought to acknowledge the post-Modern break while still defining a position from which to make abstract art—like Peter Halley, who went on record in the 1980s with the idea that his works were not really abstract paintings but simulations of them. Modernist abstraction in its heyday was carried along by a flooding sense of onrushing inevitability that bestowed upon it a feverish charisma, but Halley's paintings arose in a less defined situation. Their intentions and meanings may reflect those of Modernist abstraction but do not actually embody them. New meanings rarely intended in the Modernist period—of irony, criticism, humor, and social reference—hover around these works, distancing and diminishing the intensity of the Modernist appeal to "pure" form.

This simulationist idea overlaps somewhat with the wave of quotational work of the 1980s and since, in which artists seemingly arbitrarily recapitulate and scramble sequences already transacted in the past, implying a model of history in which Modernist linearity goes nuts: the line of progress that had previously advanced only forward now curves unpredictably back on itself, repeats certain of its earlier stages both chaotically and obsessively, drifts, skips, jumps, and circles about as if there were no longer a future to advance into. The practitioners of quotational art tend to be acutely aware of the Modernist model of history as something outmoded yet still exerting an archetypal presence. Pat Steir's *The Brueghel Series (a Vanitas of Style),* for example, involves a compaction of linear history into a single plane, suggesting both the neo-pre-Modern eternal present and, more strongly, the sense that history is a completed icon. The linear advance has crashed into a wall and flattened out.

Some quotational artists, such as Mike Bidlo, have seemed like worshippers in a ruined church, gathering Modernist memorabilia from the ashes. Others, like Sherrie Levine, have acted as subverters of the faith, wary lest it be merely playing dead, insisting that what is over is over. Yet often in this work, the linear view of history still seems powerful. There is a kind of fear of it in the air, of the possibility of its return, and the artists have a purifying goal, as if trying to free us from the threat of its resurgence. At moments, it seemed almost as if the climactic end of linear history could be constituted precisely by this stalling of Modernism's forward urge into a self-absorbed reflection on itself. Quotational art can even be seen as fulfilling the Hegelian prediction of self-realization as the culmination of

history; so this work has something apocalyptic
about it, and draws its strength from the old myth
even as it dismantles it. The scramblers' puritanical
intensity, too, has something of the Modernist fer-
vor, as if they were carrying out Modernism's secret intention in the very act of refuting it. In this
sense, quotationalism is a true successor to Minimal-
ism and Conceptualism, both of which also drew
their intensity from the idea that they were taking
Modernism to the mat. The scrambled-line model is
a kind of period to Modernism, or a burial of it,
marking an end, not a beginning.

The current phase of post-Modern realization, as
culture feels its way into the future without the Hegelian map to guide it, is so-called multiculturalism.
Here too, however, the Hegelian structure may have
been revised but not thoroughly abandoned. Betrayed and excluded peoples, for example, have
sometimes tried to turn the tables without changing
the game; having been so vulnerable themselves,
they want their former masters at their mercy, at
least ideologically. The revisionist model of history
proposed by Cheikh Anta Diop, a Senegalese writer
who died in 1986 and who is currently enormously
influential in the African diaspora, is one such mani-
festation. Essentially, Diop preserves the Hegelian
idea of hierarchy and centrality but reverses the hierarchy's top and bottom; by the simple argument that
ancient Egypt was in fact a black African society (a
troubled hypothesis in terms of the evidence[3]), by
ignoring the ancient Near Eastern input into the beginning of the complex that we call civilization, and

other such tactics, he can assert that to black Africa belong the laurels of creating civilization in all its modes—artistic, scientific, governmental, literary, religious, mathematical, spiritual. It is European scholars, in the interest of European cultural hegemony, who have robbed Africa of the credit, falsely attributing it to the ancient Greeks.[4] In other words, Diop does not question the Hegelian idea of more and less advanced cultures. He merely reverses the hierarchy, preserving the idea of a single world-historical civilization in advance of all others, but revealing that civilization as having been not European but African all along.

The broad availability of this simple strategy is demonstrated by the pan-Indianist position advanced by the Indian author Paramesh Choudhary, who argues, with stunning parallelism to Diop, that in fact ancient Egyptian culture was merely a colony sent out from the Indus Valley, the Bronze Age culture of India.[5] The ancient Egyptians, then, were not black, not even African; they were Indian. In fact, Choudhary enthusiastically argues—with approaches to evidence that often parallel Diop's—that all of North Africa as far as Mauritania, along with most of the ancient Near East, showed no trace of civilization until they, too, were colonized from the Indus Valley.

These arguments do not fully qualify, of course, as revisionist models of history, since they leave the structure and dynamics of the Hegelian model in place, only assigning the players new roles. Neither can pan-Africanism or pan-Indianism be regarded as

truly multicultural, though they are sometimes presented as such; they are simply inverse forms of Eu-
rocentrism.

Genuinely multicultural proposals attempt to
eliminate—or at least to diminish—the elements of
hierarchy and centrality rather than simply to fill in
the blanks with new names. Because revolutions,
however, can never begin with a clean slate but are
always born from the past, it is perhaps inevitable
that even the most genuinely multicultural approach
contains residual elements of Hegelianism. Hegel
had thought the next age would see the world Prus-
sianized, and that that would constitute the end of
history. Nowadays, we see the next age not as a
Prussian ordering or homogenization of worldwide
culture, but as a pluralistic globalization of it. Supposedly, cultures will reach some stable interaction
that will balance and respect their differences. But
behind the very idea of achieving a stable stage of
time lies the unspoken suggestion that this levelled
or non-hierarchical, multicultural global civilization
will in fact constitute the famous end of history—the
millennium predicted by Hegel. Merely by saying,
as we look back over the last decade, that progress
has been made in the transition from quotationalism
to multiculturalism, we show that the idea of linear
progress is still in place in our consciousness, though
the linearity that it assumes is no longer a tight line
but one that spreads out like a broad river delta yet
still advances toward its end, where many channels
empty into the sea.

This is not so much a revision of history as an

abrogation of it. To say that all rivers will melt into the sea—that history is over—is simply to erase the line from the page, leaving an ahistorical blank. Such a situation, of course, is unlikely to occur, not only because the achievement of some still point of stasis always seems more a theoretical possibility than a practical one, but because multiculturalism in particular is a complexification of the picture, rather than a simplification of it. It cannot be an end, for it contains countless unresolved themes and issues. If it is to be anything, it will certainly be a turning toward a new dynamic with its own benefits and dangers. The contentious rise of new co-optive moves in the hierarchical mode, such as pan-Africanism and pan-Indianism, already demonstrates this.

The difficulty of getting beyond models of history that are merely lightly disguised power trips has something to do with the appeal of the simple explanatory principle. The circular, the spiral, and the straight-line models of history all rest on primary shapes; they all bear something of the Platonic ideal of metaphysical simplicity, and in this they parallel the ideology of geometric abstract art—the goal of appearing to unveil the secret inmost structures of the universe. The most prominent multicultural formulation of history also demonstrates this temptation. In this view, instead of one big History moving across the page of otherwise unhistoricized time, several smaller histories all cruise along together, albeit with different languages, skin colors, and cultural styles. Instead of one deeply etched line crossing the page, a series of more lightly inscribed lines run parallel. Surely this view is a big improvement over the Eurocentric one. Yet it still incorporates all the linearity and one-directionality of the Modernist model, only rendering it more pluralistic; it might almost be a magnified view of the Modernist line, revealing the microscopic components that the naked eye sees as a single trace.

A model which might express our moment of realization more accurately is an array of dissimilar line fragments flung randomly down on the page, some intersecting others, some paralleling others, some more or less isolated. We are entering a period when every ethnic group or bonding group or community of taste or belief will write and rewrite its own fragment of history, and probably in many conflicting versions. A more or less unconnected array of micro-narratives will replace, for a time, the single meta-narrative. If this process goes on uncontrolled— without, that is, the premature imposition of a new meta-narrative—a general cohesiveness or sense of framework or of mutual relationship may naturally emerge, like a pattern appearing among leaves on the ground after enough of them have fallen. A more copious, ample meta-narrative may begin to articulate itself, made up of the interaction of the many fragments rather than imposing itself upon them.

There are enormous problems to this hopeful idea, however. One has already been illustrated: the danger that different groups, not content with writing their own micro-narratives, will try to take over the meta-narrative in the old style that they had suffered from, as the pan-Africanists and pan-Indianists are already attempting. Another problem may be that we will look at the emerging pattern not merely as leaves but as tea leaves, providing interpretive readings to form a meta-narrative before one is ready. It may also turn out that various peoples, writing their mini-histories in their separate cubicles in the scriptorium of the world, will use different historiographic conventions, rules of evidence, methodologies, and so on. At the end of a few years, they may be writing history in such different ways that a new meta-narrative cannot be conceived to encompass them all without becoming indiscriminately accommodating to contradiction.

On reflection, though, this last may be the least of the problems we face—less a problem than a temporary solution. Why not let the world breathe for a while without a meta-narrative constricting it into a narrow space that is claimed as ultimate? Why not let it feel its way into the future without those totalizing, globalizing, universalizing, redemptionist myths which have so much in common with religious prophecies? Note, though, that this acceptance of a suspended moment is not the same thing as saying that history is over and anything goes. Post-Modernism is not an anarchic or nihilistic trashing of access to a sense of the coherence, framework, direction, or meaning of history. It is a remapping of the terrain for a new and difficult era. It may well be that History is over—but histories endure.

NOTES

1. Or with something like what Dave Hickey has referred to as the "dimestore sublime" in "Polke in America—The Non-Returnable Flounder and the Dime-Store Sublime," *Parkett* no. 30, 1991, pp. 86–91.

2. Arthur C. Danto, "Post-Historical Abstract Painting," *Tema Celeste,* Autumn 1991, p. 55.

3. See, for example, Frank Snowden, Jr., *Before Color Prejudice: The Ancient View of Blacks,* Cambridge, MA: Harvard University Press, 1983, pp. 7–8.

4. See Cheikh Anta Diop, *Civilization and Barbarism: An Authentic Anthropology,* Brooklyn, NY: Lawrence Hill Books, 1991; and Cheikh Anta Diop, *The African Origin of Civilization: Myth or Reality,* Brooklyn, NY: Lawrence Hill Books, 1974.

5. See Paramesh Choudhary, *Indian Origin of the Chinese Nation,* Calcutta: Dasgupta and Company, Private, Ltd., 1990.

The Romance:
A Paradox

The self is created by its apprehension of an other. The other is created by its distinction from a self. They create each other and sustain each other's existence. Each makes the other what it is.

The self cannot be itself unless it stands against what is not-self. Not-self is needed to make self self. Therefore not-self is in self. It is its necessary condition and its negative essence.

The other is not other except in its difference from self. It is brought into existence by the self's apprehension of that difference. The other and the self are simultaneous. They come into existence at the same instant and recreate one another at each succeeding instant.

There cannot be self without other; there cannot be other without self. They exist only and always in a secret embrace. They are a mutually dependent, eternally interlinked pair.

Self and other are two; the relation of difference between them is a third; the difference of each of them from the relation of difference constitutes a fourth and a fifth; and so on ad infinitum. Thus the gaps that separate the self from the other are infinite.

The bonds that join the self and the other are also infinite. Their reciprocal necessity flashes endlessly back and forth between them, like the caresses of their embrace.

Each, in its selfsameness, knows itself and is unknown to the other. Each, in its difference, is known to the other and unknown to itself.

Insofar as the other is unknown it is known; insofar as it is known it is unknown. The other is other because it is unknown. The other is known because it is known to be other. It is known by negative implications of the self.

Insofar as self is unknown it is known. It is known as self only by its distinction from the other, which as other is unknown. It is known insofar as it is

different from an unknown. It is known by an un-
knowable difference. It is unknowably known.

It is not merely that the other is a mystery *to* the self;
it is that the other is a mystery *of* the self.

Sameness is self without other and hence without
self. Difference is not-self, with otherness and hence
with self. Sameness is sleep, nonentity, abyss, bliss.
Difference is awakeness, entity, form, anxiety.

Sameness is made sameness by its difference from
difference, as self is made self by its separation from
an other. Sameness contains difference as its hidden
essence as the self contains the other as its unknow-
able known.

Sameness is unutterable. If two things are the same
then any predication between them is tautologous.
Difference is unutterable. If two things are different
then any predication between them is meaningless.

If a thing is itself by reason of selfsameness it is not
a self since it is not defined by a difference. If a thing
is itself by reason of difference it is different from
itself and the same as not-self.

If a thing is both the same and different then it is two things. If a thing is two things then each of these two things, also both the same as itself and different from an other, is two more things. And so on ad infinitum.

Sameness lies at the heart of difference. Difference is the irrevocable condition of sameness.

The self fears the other, thinking that otherness will overwhelm it and cause it to cease being itself. Yet it is the other alone that compels the self always to be itself.

If it wishes to escape the other, the self can only sink into it, fusing with it so that neither self nor other remains to be seen. If it wishes to absorb the other into itself and enrich itself through otherness, the self, drawn out of its limits, can only force the other into new forms of otherness.

The self can never reach the other and can never do without it.

The self's love of and need for the other is matched only by its hatred of and repulsion from it. The other is the eternally elusive beloved and the eternally pursuing enemy.

The self reaches for the veil of the other trembling to see itself. The other slips beneath the skin of the self and becomes its desire and its terror.

Pursued by the other, the self flees it through all nature, begetting in its flight the infinite forms of selfhood and of otherness.

Yearning for the other, the self pursues it through all nature, annihilating the countless forms in its desire to leap into the abyss.

Change is the procreation of the self and the other. The infinite is begotten through their sameness and their difference.

APPENDIX A

The Global Issue

When asked why he wished to be buried upside down,
Diogenes replied, "Down will soon be up."

"Writing before the exhibition," I remarked in the catalogue
of the Centre Pompidou's *Magiciens de la terre* show in Paris
last summer [1989], "I do not know (nor may I after) how
well or badly it will fulfill its post-Modern agenda." Now the
exhibition has happened, occasioning a hail of mostly negative
criticism rather similar in premise to the attacks (including
my own) on the Museum of Modern Art's *"Primitivism" in
20th Century Art* show in New York in 1984. One has to be
sympathetic to the counter-hegemonic impulse behind this
criticism of *Magiciens de la terre*. Still, in the end, it misses the
point.

Like many viewers, I had problems with the show. There
were many distressing signs of residual colonial attitudes. The
title, for example, suggested a romantic tilt toward the idea
of the "native artist" as not only a magician (with the term's
suggestion of the pre-rational) but also as somehow close to
the earth (not *magiciens du monde,* but *de la terre*), as if in some
pre-civilized state of nature. The curators were understandably
motivated by a desire not to use the word "artists," in defer-
ence to the ongoing anthropological debate about whether so-
called "primitive" peoples have the ideology (essentially, in
our terms, Kantian) that makes objects "art" in our sense of
the word. Still, an aura of Rousseau and of the Noble Savage
clings round their title. And the word *magicien* really does not
express very precisely what Hans Haacke does, or Lawrence

Weiner, or Barbara Kruger, or Cheri Samba, or many others in the show, both Eastern and Western—or Northern or Southern.

The tilt toward the cliché of the earthy native was also visible in the selection and installation of the works. Despite the fact, for example, that a number of artists in India are currently attempting to work out a thoughtful conflation of Indian and Western styles and themes, the curators chose to exhibit primarily traditional, craftlike work from that country. Actually, most of the artists in *Magiciens* who might be described as cool, intellectual, and conceptual were Westerners (Weiner, Kruger, Haacke, Daniel Buren, and so on); and in general (though not without exception), the artists whose work seemed most earthy and ritualistic were non-Western (Esther Mahlangu of South Africa, Cyprien Tokoudagba of Benin, Nuche Kaji Bajrocharya of Nepal, Joe Ben Jr., a Native American sand painter, and so on). It would not have been hard to reverse, or to balance, those categories, perhaps by placing more emphasis on work that attempts to bridge the gap. (But maybe that is another show, and the next stage in the post-colonialist process.) Indeed, the curators may have intended a gesture at such a balance through the huge Richard Long mud painting in the portion of the show at La Villette— the "earthiest" piece in the exhibition, literally, and by a European artist. But as many seem to have felt, the overriding presence of the Long circle, which dominated everything at La Villette, smacked of hierarchy. Even more unfortunate was the aboriginal sand painting lying on the floor beneath it, as if conquered or raped.

More could be said, and has been said by others, to indicate how the curators failed to arrive at a fully post-colonialist show. Not least would be the atrocious catalogue statements by the curators themselves, with their talk of spirituality implying universals they may not have intended, and their rather clumsy, gung-ho enthusiasms. But for all this, it nevertheless seems to me that the generally negative press reaction to *Magiciens de la terre* was mistaken. (Though I wrote what the curators called the keynote statement in the catalogue, I made no curatorial contribution to the exhibition, and have no ongoing connection with the Pompidou. My defense of the show is based on my belief in its premises, not in the details of the curation.)

Part of the reason for the often hostile reaction to *Magiciens* may have been the fact that it was not seen in the United States and the *"Primitivism"* show was not seen in Europe. One cannot really understand *Magiciens* without thinking of what the *"Primitivism"* show meant in terms of history and society.

It was in a moment of attitudinal change that the *"Primitivism"* show appeared, like a holding action for classical Modernism. There was the Kantian doctrine of universal quality again; there was the Hegelian view that history is a story of Europeans leading dark-skinned peoples toward spiritual realization; there was the sense of mainstream and periphery. The fact that so-called "primitive" art resembled Western advanced art seemed to be attributed primarily not to the incontestable fact that the Western artists had imitated "primitive" works, but to the idea of an underlying affinity between Western artists and "primitives" that demonstrated the universality of the Modernist canon. The colonized nations were called upon to testify to the superiority of the colonizers. It was a kind of police action.

Magiciens was conceived in the midst of the widespread controversy over the *"Primitivism"* show. The hope it embodied was to find a post-colonialist way to exhibit the works of First and Third World artists together, a way that would involve no projections about hierarchy, or about mainstream and periphery, or about history having a goal. Works by 50 Western and 50 non-Western artists would be exhibited in a neutral, loose, unsystematic way that would not imply transcultural value judgments. The exhibition would be superficially similar to *"Primitivism"* in that it too would exhibit First and Third World artists side by side in a major Western museum. But where *"Primitivism"* had left the "primitive" works anonymous and undated, *Magiciens* would treat them exactly as it treated Western pieces. Where *"Primitivism"* had been Eurocentric and hierarchic, *Magiciens* would level all hierarchies, letting the artworks appear without any fixed ideological framework around them. Where *"Primitivism"* presented "primitive" works as footnotes to their Western Modernist imitations, *Magiciens* would choose each work by what appeared to its curators to be its interest as itself, not by its value at illustrating something other than itself. (The curators' taste, it seemed to me, functioned in the selection process as a kind of random element.) Where *"Primitivism"* came equipped with a huge, hectoring catalogue enforcing the curators' view of virtually everything in the show, *Magiciens* just put the stuff out there unexplained, or, rather, untamed by explanation. As for the idea of a center, *Magiciens,* at least in the catalogue, would make a gesture toward dismissing it. Each artist was given two pages in the volume; on each spread was a small map that showed the artist's home as the center of the globe.

Perhaps the key fact is that the two exhibitions embodied radically different ideas of history. *"Primitivism"* was still based on the Hegelian myth of Western cultures leading the rest of the world forward; *Magiciens* was the epitaph of this view, and of the Kantian idea of the universal value judgment. If history has no goal, then there can be no basis on which to claim that one culture is more advanced toward the goal than any other. Suddenly, each culture is simply the most advanced example of its type. Each culture has an equal claim to be just where it is.

The *"Primitivism"* show was based on a belief in universally valid quality judgments, particularly those made by the curators. The *Magiciens* show hoped to be able to acknowledge that value judgments are not innate or universal but conditioned by social context, and hence that they only really fit works emerging from the same context. This thought does not mark the end of the idea of quality, only its relativization. When one walked through *Magiciens,* instead of automatically thinking this or that was good or bad, one might be provoked to attend to the limitations of one's ideas of good and bad: to confront the fact that often one was looking at objects for which one had no criteria except some taken from a completely different, and possibly completely irrelevant, arena. The absence of a scholarly catalogue left the viewer confronted simply with the works and the bewilderment they might produce.

Criticism of *Magiciens* came from both the right and the left. To rightist critics, the show seemed a destroyer of Modernism. The curators had given up the Western claim to being a more advanced civilization; they had given up our long-claimed right to judge other cultures by our own standards, and to treat these judgments as somehow objective. This anxiety must underlie the unpublished remark of a prominent British critic that *Magiciens* marked the end of Western civilization—as if Western civilization were constituted precisely by the claim to hegemony; as if yielding that claim, one yielded all.

Critics approaching from the left expressed unhappiness at how depoliticized the show was. They questioned the motives of the institution, suspecting it of, among other things, attempting to recapture French cultural claims to global relevance. They brought up the tradition of French colonialism, sometimes implying that the show might better have transpired in Kinshasa or Djibouti—places where, unfortunately, it probably would not have affected much the way the Western art world operates. They questioned the idea of introducing these artists into the Western market system, like innocent lambs being led to the slaughter. They questioned the imposition of bourgeois individualist values on these artists from supposedly communal societies. They spoke of *Magiciens* as if it were *"Primitivism."*

The bone everyone has been picking—right, left, or centrist—is the lame curation. The show didn't add up in so many ways, despite the good sense of its underlying premises. I don't argue that point. (In fact, I feel that the show's inconsistencies saved it from the rigidity of a single framework of value.) What I am defending is an idea that I think was never really in question and that I doubt anyone wants directly to attack. All the criticism of the show that I have seen fails to confront the monumental fact that this was the first major exhibition consciously to attempt to discover a post-colonialist way to exhibit objects together. It was a major event in the social history of art, not in its esthetic history. *Magiciens* opened the door of the long-insular and hermetic Western art world to non-Western artists. The question is not really whether the people who opened the door had gravy on their jackets, or slipped and fell as they were opening it. The question is this and only this: as we enter the global village of the '90s, would any of us *really* rather that the door remain closed?

Some of the criticism of the show was honorably motivated

by a compassionate concern for the Third World artists. This concern arises understandably from a skepticism about whether the door is really open, how far it's open, and how long it will stay open. It has happened before that the Western art market, seeking new goods, has elevated a previously peripheral group to the mainstream and, when it didn't work out financially, ejected them again. (One thinks, for example, of the Mexican muralists of the '30s and of the graffiti artists of the early '80s.) But this time greater forces than those of the market seem to be mandating a reassessment of the boundaries of contemporary art. In the next few years we shall see whether down becomes up. It may be that now the deck of cards of Western art history has been thrown irrevocably into the air—that there are unknown elements in the game now, elements not yet under any particular control.

ART/artifact

What Makes Something Art?

The following remarks were delivered at a Center for African Art colloquium in New York City on April 11, 1988. Susan Vogel, director of the Center had mounted an exhibition titled ART/artifact, *which was intended partly to investigate some of the issues raised by the ideological conflict between the "Primitivism" show and* Magiciens de la terre. *Susan Vogel, Arthur Danto, James Faris, Enid Schildkrout, and I discussed the question, "What makes something art?" My talk was made from notes and does not represent a finished text.*

It has been traditional in our culture at least since Kant to assume that the category of the artwork has something to do with the category of the beautiful. Of course many artworks do; but it seems that they need not. There are things which are beautiful but which are not art—such as a sunset—and things which are art but which are not beautiful—such as Joseph Beuys' *Fat Chair*. To narrow the category of the beautiful, to limit it to things made by people, as Kant struggles to do, does not solve the problem. There still are beautiful things— such as a handsomely designed automobile hubcap or glass bottle—which are not art, and there are still non-beautiful things which are. Evidently, the category of the art object has nothing essential to do with the category of the beautiful. In the '70s everyone knew that; in the '80s the question returned.

A related but more sophisticated approach which goes back at least to Roger Fry early in this century, and is echoed in Susan Vogel's interesting catalogue essay for this show, holds that if a thing has significant or expressive form, it is to be called art. The term "expressive intent" is often used for this idea, but again there are problems in proposing it as an actual definition.

To begin with, there are many things which have expressive form but which are not in practice called art. As early as some Cro-Magnon flaked tools from around 20,000 BC, one finds examples that are made much more finely than they need to be to get their jobs done; a care has been lavished on them that goes far beyond a functional intent. This care can only be accounted for as an expressive intent. Yet we do not therefore call these things art. Or consider fabric design, or any kind of design: such activities clearly involve expressive intent, yet we do not therefore call them art. A temper tantrum, for that matter, involves expressive intent—or love-making—but that does not make them performance art.

On the other hand, there are things which seem to lack expressive form or intent but which *are* called art. Duchamp's snow shovel Readymade, for example, according to his repeated insistence, was meant to be as far from any expressive intention as he could manage, to have no relation to his esthetic taste or his personal expressiveness at all; and its form, clearly, is functional, not expressive. That was the point of it—to show that expressive intention is not necessary for art. A row of bricks on the floor by Carl Andre is similarly designed to negate ideas of expressive form or intent; yet of course it is called art.

If one replies that a denial of expressive intent is an expressive intent of another sort—that Duchamp, for example, expressed the negation of expression—then we must allow that all human activity embodies expressive intentions; in that case, the definition has not separated the category of art from that of other things made or done by humans. Finally, it seems that when one is talking about the way things look, one is

talking not about art but about design, a quality which artworks exhibit in a huge and contradictory range of types,
presences, and negations.

One serious problem with any definition of art which
stresses esthetic or expressive qualities is that such a definition
eliminates much of what has been called art, and influential art
at that, for the last seventy years or so; esthetic qualities and
expressive intentions are more or less irrelevant to Duchamp's
snow shovel, urinal, and comb; to Andre's straight lines of
bricks or bales of hay or his floors covered with steel squares;
to Lawrence Weiner's exhibition of a wall stained with water
or his pieces involving words on the wall; to Allan Kaprow's
pile of used tires; to Hans Haacke's Shapolsky piece or his
various South Africa pieces; and to countless other works of
20th-century art. If you hold to an esthetic or expressive
definition, then, you are going to have to reject much of 20th-
century art, and are you really willing to do that? To cut
yourself off from the meanings of your own time like that? I'm
not.

Arthur Danto, in an interesting catalogue essay, argues
somewhat differently, declaring himself to be, as in certain
other of his writings, thinking from a Hegelian beginning. At
one point he writes, "To be a work of art, I have argued, is
to embody a thought, to have a content, to express a meaning." While I regard this as a welcome shift of emphasis from
form to content, and to the artwork as a philosophical object,
I think that it fails to distinguish artworks from certain other
groups of objects, including religious icons and advertise-
ments. Elsewhere Danto refers to the Hegelian idea that the
artwork carries such intensity of meaning as to indicate that it
participates in the realm of spirit.

This, too, I think, is something that we often mean when
we use the word art. But again it fails to describe the whole
category of things that are called art and also to set that category off clearly from certain others. For one thing, the definition seems to apply to religious icons as much as, or more
than, to artworks. For another, there are things that we regard
as participating in spirit which we do not call art—such as
certain books of philosophy or mathematics or science, certain
heroic or self-sacrificial gestures or acts, and the sublime in

nature. Finally, since really only what we call great art is regarded as accomplishing that sense of the immanence of Spirit,
this definition cannot recognize that there is such a thing as
failed art or mediocre or uninspired art. But, clearly, we regard
many of the things to which we apply the word art as mediocre and uninspired, as falling short of the realm of the spirit;
yet we still call them art.

If the criterion of expressive intent seems too narrow, the
criterion of content seems too broad. I believe that any and
every object made by a human expresses or embodies a
thought, an idea, a concept. So this criterion does not seem to
me to distinguish art objects from cultural objects in general.
I would regard art objects as a sub-set of the larger set of things
which involve a thought, an idea, a concept. This definition,
like that based on expressive form, requires us to say that the
word "art" is being used incorrectly in many, perhaps most,
of the cases in which it is used. But as long as the word works
as a communicative tool there is no privileged ground from
which such a judgment could be established.

Others, such as the Wittgensteinian philosopher Timothy
Binkley, have suggested a less demanding criterion. Whatever
is called art, says Binkley, is art, since to be art means exactly
nothing except that the word art is applied. As the usages of a
word change, so do the boundaries of the category. Something
which is not called art one day may be called art the next; other
things on which the title of art has been conferred may have
it withdrawn. Among all the entities in the category, no unifying element can be found which would serve as a defining trait
except that the same word is applied to all, as the same family
name is applied to people manifestly different from one another. The list of things to which we apply the word art would
contain some objects that involve expressive intent, others that
are specifically designed to negate expressive intent, some that
aspire to the realm of the spirit, others that either spurn or fall
short of it. In this view there is no property of the object itself
which makes it art or non-art; it is made art by being designated as art by the art system and, as our century has shown
us, anything at all may so be designated, from a blank canvas
to a can of human excrement to an unaltered pile of unhewn
stones in a forest.

But the idea that something is made art simply and only by being designated as art needs expanding. There is no real difference, for example, between linguistic designation and designation by context, or between those and other types of designation such as the maker's signature on an object, its exhibition in an art museum, its purchase by a collector, its mention and critique in an art magazine, its listing in an art catalogue, and so on.

This is why the argument either for or against designating art simply by naming something art seems to me now to be less important than it has sometimes been thought to be—by me as well as by others. Danto, in his catalogue essay, points out that the ancient Greeks had no precise word for art, yet who would deny that they had art? The implication is that linguistic designation is irrelevant. But of course, as I have argued above, the lexical differentiation of art from other things is not the only form of differentiation. In Homeric times, the concept of inspiration set the artist off from the artisan. By the late 6th century BC, artists—not artisans—signed their works, another form of designation by language. By Pheidias' day, Athens had an art museum, unconnected with religion, which provided a differentiating context equivalent to a lexical distinction. Thus, the concept art was separated from other concepts such as religion in a number of ways, linguistic, social, and methodological, among others.

This somewhat loosened Wittgensteinian approach may be the only one that will encompass all the things we call art and exclude the things we don't. Still, it lacks satisfaction in that it leaves no room for feeling and gives no account of *why* we call certain things art and not others. It accounts for the things called art simply by noting that they are called art. Its reductivist purism is tautological, like a piece of Minimalist sculpture.

To go one step further, one would have to ask whether the fact that certain things are called art does not itself carry additional meanings. At the very least, it must mean that one relates to the object differently from the way one would if it were called something else. So the designation as art creates a little realm of specialized feelings. Within this realm there are different inhabitants, some conflicting, which provide a map of the currents of feeling in our culture: expressiveness and form, awe and the sublime, tough-mindedness and industrial materials. It is the variations in the pantheon from culture to culture that are meaningful, as a kind of psychoanalysis or a taking of the temperature of a culture at a given moment. One thing we mean when we call something art is that we confer honor on it. The fact then, that about fifty years ago, Western culture decided to call African and other tribal objects art is meaningful socially, but its meaning speaks about the attitudes of Western culture, not about the objects themselves.

The fact that we designate something as art means that it is art for us, but says nothing about what it is in itself or for other people. Once we realize that the quest for essences is an archaic religious quest, there is no reason why something should not be art for one person or culture and non-art for another. In fact, if linguistic designation, or some similar mode of designating, is the only criterion that makes something art or not-art, then it is not only Duchamp's Readymades and similar things which are art by designation: really, everything that is art is art by designation. There is no other way to be art.

In this view, then, the process by which we have treated tribal functional objects as art is analogous to the process by which we have made our own functional objects, such as snow shovels, bricks, and tires, into art. Their status is that of found objects which we have contextualized as art with the art system in general acting as designating artist. The question whether these objects were art in their original African contexts is a question of how they were culturally designated at the time and in the place they were made, and that is a question for Africans and ethnographers to settle.

Before an object can be regarded as art pure and simple, however, I think it must have freed itself from the matrix of religion and rite, or rather the receiver's mind must have so freed itself. Designating something as a salvational or magical object is such a strong projection of meaning and emotion that one who is in its grip does not see beyond it, in fact must not. To see beyond that meaning—to regard the object for its formal qualities or, say, for its social implications—would be to negate its religious sense and void its magical power. Religious objects of the European Middle Ages, then, may not have been understood as art in their day but are so now, by us who are no longer encompassed in the matrix of medieval religious belief.

* * *

The debate over the relationship between Western and so-called primitive art is surprisingly controversial and acrimonious. Perhaps that is because it is the only context anymore which brings up the question, "What is art?" In the past, that question was brought up by Duchamp's snow shovel, by Pollock's drip paintings when it was discovered that a monkey could do them about as well, by Klein's monochromes, by Warhol's Brillo boxes, and so on. Then, sometime around 1970, the question just stopped being asked. The boundaries of what had been called art had been stretched to the point where it seemed silly even to bring it up. Some assumed that art had simply died at some point or other along the way. There are, for example, people who watched faithfully and with interest until the drip paintings, and drew the line there; others who watched till the *Brillo Boxes* and drew the line there; others who in the high spirit of budding pluralism just let it all happen.

The question didn't really come up again until the exhibition *"Primitivism" in 20th Century Art* at New York's Museum of Modern Art in 1984. At that time various of us observed that the tribal objects were not understood as art in their own contexts and questioned whether it was not an act of cultural imperialism to call them art in our context without any apparent concern for the feelings and intentions of the people who made them and the people for whom they were made. Through some adjustments in our perceptions, we may become able to begin practicing anthropology as cultural critique, not forcing objects from other cultures into our categories, but rather allowing those objects to raise questions about ours, what they are really for and how their situation is limited.

To say that it is its designation as art—either through language or context, or otherwise—which makes something art is next door to saying that art is a stance taken toward an object either by someone separately or by the culture in general. One such stance is to view an object with appreciative regard to its formal qualities or with regard to its expressive qualities of whatever kind.

The exhibition *ART/artifact* presented African objects in four different settings—an "art gallery," an "art museum," a "curio room," and a diorama installation—and asked the viewer to consider whether the nature of the objects was altered by the change in the nature of the setting. From a certain point of view the answer seemed an obvious No: the objects remained themselves, whatever they are or were, regardless of the situation in which one looked at them. This is a point of view that tends to see objects as separate entities with specific identities that dwell within them as essences and resist the tug of ambient events. Such a point of view is characteristic of Anglo-American thinking, but less so of Continental European thought which, still saturated with the totalizing influence of Hegel, tends to see all things as implicated with one another so that when one element of the web changes the others must change in response. From this point of view, an object is not simply self-identical but is constituted at least in part by its place in the larger context of things; the different contextualizations of an object may indeed be regarded as affecting its nature. Whether we emphasize the reality of the individual entity or the reality of the surrounding web in which it is constituted, it is clear in either case that our *experience* of the object will be changed by changes in context, and it is questionable whether the object can be regarded otherwise than as it is experienced.

In asking, then, "What makes something art?," we implicitly suggest that either context or some element in the nature of the thing in itself makes the difference. It's useful to bear in mind the Socratic and Wittgensteinian method of regarding the usage of the word in seeking its meaning. The Socratic idea was that if we regard the various usages of a word, we will find some element that is common to them all but not to other things and will isolate that element as the essence which defines the category of things referred to by the word. The problem is, of course, that Socrates found that in practice he never came up with an element common to the various usages of the words he investigated. Wittgenstein also advised that the search for an essential definition will come up empty.

The search for an essential definition, after all, is posited on a belief in the existence of essences in things. It is, in other words, an essentially religious type of quest for unchanging verities—a quest which our culture has not much emphasized in recent years. It is perhaps only in the art discourse, in fact, that this archaic quest for essence is still prominent, a fact which will remind us how much we still regard art with anachronistic religious overtones that derive from its ancient aura as an arm of religion.

Finally, the quest for an essential definition, which is simply the meaning of a word in an absolute sense, has inner contradictions. Most obviously, such a definition would by nature be unchanging, and since the history of languages shows us that usages change, usage must drift over time from the original denotation of a word and become attached to what is, presumably, a false definition. But if a word is being used in a certain way and manages to communicate in that way, there can be no ground from which to say it is being used wrongly.

INDEX

169